INCREDIBLE BHARAT

VISION FOR VIKASIT BHARAT

MS. RESHEL BRETNY FERNANDES
Young International national author and orator,
Kittur Rani chennamma state awardee 2025

TANEESHA PUBLISHING

ISBN : 9788199862517
Edition : First, March 2026
Title : Incredible Bharat Vision for Vikasit Bharat
Author : Ms. Reshel Bretny Fernandes

Published by

TANEESHA PUBLISHING

An Imprint of **Taneesha and Prachi NextGen Publication**

Registered Office: Sunil Complex, 2nd Floor, Vijay Nagar,
Western Kutchery Road, Meerut - 250002, Uttar Pradesh, India
Website : www.taneeshapublishing.com
E-mail : support@tpnextpub.com
Phone : 0121 453 0364

Printed by :
Manipal Technologies Limited, Bengaluru - 560001, Karnataka

Remembering the visionary leadership of

Sardar Vallabhbhai Patel

EKTA DIVAS

PREFACE

Bharat our pride not just with the geographical beauty but stands unique with the message of Vasudhaiva Kutumbakam the strings of beauty enhances the worldly admiration of gaining the utmost confidence towards striving ahead unified in the ties of incredibility.

The focus is on past present and future leading the journey of making goals into reality with desired options for the success through diversity as our strength at global scenario with the ethical serenity and focusing on strategic ideas.

The youth and citizens are the pillars shaping the society of tomorrow who engage themselves into a deep understanding of what is needed in order to shape the society at levels of development.

In an incredible society it is our responsibility as the citizens to fulfill the aspirations needed to unify among differences and have the glory in segmenting to understand the beauty that Bharat stands for!!Incredible Bharat a vision for VIKASIT BHARAT makes a remarkable attempt to signify the need of uplifting nation building and a sense of feeling that leads further for EK BHARAT STRESTH BHARAT

Ms. Reshel Bretny Fernandes

06.02.2026

ACKNOWLEDGEMENT

I thank almighty for giving me the strength to pen down this book. I thank my parents and my family members for the support and blessings.

I thank members of Bharatiya Janata party and leaders who have supported me always.

I thank Disha Bharat, samartha bharata, Thinkers Forum and other organisations for the support always.

I thank each and everyone for supporting me always.

Bharat very essence of the nation's historical, social, and cultural fabric. It speaks to the remarkable ability of a civilization to assimilate, accommodate, and celebrate a multitude of ethnicities, religions, languages, and traditions within a single, unified national identity. The historical narrative of Bharat is intrinsically interwoven with the threads of diversity. From the ancient Indus Valley Civilization, a melting pot of various communities and practices, to the successive waves of migrations and invasions that shaped its demographics, the land has consistently served as a crucible for cultural exchange and synthesis. The Mauryan Empire, with its vast reach and diverse administrative structures, further solidified this trend, fostering a sense of shared governance across disparate regions. The subsequent centuries witnessed the rise and fall of numerous kingdoms and empires, each contributing its unique flavor to the cultural mosaic of Bharat. The Gupta period, often hailed as a golden age, saw a flourishing of arts, sciences, and literature, drawing inspiration from various indigenous and foreign sources. The medieval era brought with it the influence of Islamic cultures, resulting in a vibrant fusion of architectural styles, musical traditions, and philosophical thought.The arrival of European powers in the colonial period presented both challenges and opportunities for the concept of unity in diversity. While colonial rule often exploited existing social divisions for political gain, it also inadvertently fostered a sense of shared resistance and a collective yearning for self-determination, ultimately culminating in the Indian independence movement.

The geographical landscape of Bharat has profoundly shaped its diverse cultural identities. The towering Himalayas in the north, the fertile Gangetic plains, the arid Thar Desert, the coastal regions of the south, and the dense forests of the northeast have each fostered distinct ways of life, languages, and traditions. These geographical variations have not only influenced agricultural practices, architectural styles, and social customs but have also contributed to the development of unique regional identities. The Indo-Gangetic plain, for instance, with its abundant water resources and fertile soil, has historically been a center of agricultural activity and population density. This region has witnessed the rise and fall of numerous empires and has been a melting pot of diverse cultures and religions. The Himalayan region, on the other hand, with its rugged terrain and challenging climate, has fostered a culture of resilience and self-sufficiency. The people of this region have developed unique agricultural practices, such as terrace farming, and have preserved their distinct cultural traditions. The coastal regions of Bharat, with their long coastlines and access to maritime trade routes, have been centers of commerce and cultural exchange. These regions have been influenced by various foreign cultures, including those of the Middle East, Southeast Asia, and Europe. The result has been a vibrant mix of architectural styles, culinary traditions, and religious practices. Similarly, the arid Thar Desert has fostered a culture of adaptation and resourcefulness. The people of this region have developed unique water conservation techniques and have preserved their distinct nomadic traditions. The geographical diversity of Bharat has thus contributed to the richness and complexity of its cultural landscape, fostering a sense of regional pride and identity while simultaneously contributing to the overall unity of the nation. This interplay between geography and culture underscores the foundational role of the land in shaping Bharat's unique identity.

The tapestry of religions and philosophies that have flourished in Bharat is a testament to its long-standing tradition of intellectual and spiritual pluralism. Hinduism, with its diverse schools of thought and myriad deities, has been a dominant force, shaping the cultural landscape and providing a framework for social organization. Buddhism and Jainism, originating in Bharat, further enriched the spiritual landscape with their emphasis on non-violence, compassion, and self-discipline. The arrival of Islam brought with it new architectural styles, artistic traditions, and philosophical perspectives, contributing to a vibrant synthesis of cultures. Sikhism, a syncretic faith that emerged in the Punjab region, further exemplified the spirit of religious harmony and tolerance. The interaction between these diverse religious and philosophical traditions has resulted in a unique cultural synthesis, evident in various aspects of life, from art and architecture to music and literature. The Bhakti movement, for instance, transcended religious boundaries, promoting a message of love, devotion, and social equality. Sufism, with its emphasis on mystical experience and universal brotherhood, further contributed to the spirit of religious harmony. The architectural landscape of Bharat is replete with examples of this cultural synthesis, with temples, mosques, and churches coexisting harmoniously, often incorporating elements from different religious traditions. The philosophical discourse in Bharat has also been shaped by the interaction between different schools of thought, with Hindu, Buddhist, Jain, and Islamic scholars engaging in debates and discussions, enriching the intellectual landscape. This rich religious and philosophical heritage underscores the importance of tolerance, understanding, and mutual respect in maintaining the unity and integrity of Bharat. The enduring legacy of these interactions highlights the nation's capacity to embrace diverse spiritual paths while fostering a shared sense of belonging.

The linguistic diversity of Bharat is unparalleled, with hundreds of languages and dialects spoken across the country. These languages belong to different language families, including Indo-Aryan, Dravidian, Austro-Asiatic, and Tibeto-Burman, reflecting the complex history of migrations and cultural interactions that have shaped the linguistic landscape of the region. The Constitution of Bharat recognizes 22 languages as official languages, reflecting the commitment to linguistic pluralism and the recognition of the importance of language in preserving cultural identity. The linguistic diversity of Bharat is not merely a matter of different languages being spoken in different regions. It also reflects the existence of distinct literary traditions, artistic expressions, and cultural practices associated with each language. The rich literary heritage of Bharat includes ancient texts, classical poetry, folk tales, and modern novels, written in various languages, reflecting the diverse experiences and perspectives of the people of Bharat. The performing arts, including music, dance, and drama, also vary significantly across different linguistic regions, reflecting the unique cultural traditions associated with each language. The linguistic diversity of Bharat has also played a significant role in shaping its political landscape. The demand for linguistic states, based on the principle of linguistic identity, led to the reorganization of states in the mid-20th century, reflecting the recognition of the importance of language in shaping political boundaries and identities. The promotion of linguistic pluralism and the protection of linguistic rights have been important goals of the Indian government, reflecting the commitment to preserving the linguistic diversity of the nation. This commitment to linguistic diversity underscores the belief that language is not merely a means of communication but also a vital component of cultural identity and a source of national strength. The vibrant tapestry of languages woven across the nation enriches its cultural heritage and strengthens the bonds of unity.

The historical interactions between different cultures and communities in Bharat have resulted in a unique synthesis of traditions, customs, and practices. This synthesis is evident in various aspects of life, from cuisine and clothing to art and architecture. The culinary traditions of Bharat, for instance, reflect the influence of various cultures, with each region boasting its unique dishes and flavors. The use of spices, cooking techniques, and ingredients varies significantly across different regions, reflecting the diverse agricultural practices and cultural preferences of the people. The clothing styles of Bharat also reflect the influence of various cultures, with traditional garments such as sarees, dhotis, and salwar kameez varying in design, fabric, and ornamentation across different regions. The art and architecture of Bharat are replete with examples of cultural synthesis, with temples, mosques, and churches incorporating elements from different artistic traditions. The Mughal architecture, for instance, represents a fusion of Persian, Islamic, and Indian styles, resulting in iconic structures such as the Taj Mahal and Humayun's Tomb. The colonial not merely a political slogan but a reflection of the lived reality of the people of Bharat, who have historically embraced cultural exchange and synthesis. This ongoing process of cultural exchange and adaptation continues to shape the identity of Bharat, fostering a sense of shared heritage and national pride. The blended traditions stand as a testament to the nation's dynamic and evolving cultural landscape.

The historical journey of Bharat reveals a continuous negotiation and celebration of its inherent diversity. From ancient civilizations to the modern republic, the ability to accommodate and integrate varied cultures, religions, and languages has been a defining characteristic. This intricate tapestry, woven with threads of geographical influences, philosophical traditions, linguistic expressions, and cultural syntheses, showcases a civilization that has thrived on its pluralism. The challenges of maintaining unity in the face of such diversity have been significant, particularly during periods of colonial rule and social upheaval. However, the enduring commitment to inclusivity, as exemplified by the leaders of the independence movement and enshrined in the Constitution, has enabled Bharat to navigate these challenges and emerge as a vibrant and democratic nation. The concept of unity in diversity is not merely a historical artifact but a living ideal that continues to shape the identity of Bharat. It requires ongoing efforts to promote social harmony, cultural understanding, and mutual respect among its diverse communities. As Bharat continues to evolve in the 21st century, embracing its diversity will be crucial to its success and prosperity. The nation's strength lies not in homogenization but in the recognition and celebration of its multifaceted heritage, ensuring that all voices are heard and all cultures are valued. The future of Bharat depends on its ability to uphold this principle, fostering a society where diversity is not a source of division but a source of strength and resilience.

The concepts of *Vasudhaiva Kutumbakam* (the world is one family) and *Sarve Janaha Sukhino Bhavantu* (may all beings be happy) are not merely philosophical tenets, but potent guiding principles deeply embedded in the cultural and spiritual ethos of Bharat (India). These ideals, resonating through millennia of Indian thought, offer a compelling framework for fostering unity within the nation, especially in the face of its remarkable diversity. Bharat, a land of myriad languages, religions, castes, and customs, has historically navigated the complexities of its pluralism through philosophies that emphasize interconnectedness, empathy, and universal well-being. These principles provide a moral compass, encouraging citizens to transcend narrow parochial identities and embrace a broader sense of belonging. *Vasudhaiva Kutumbakam* promotes the idea that humanity is a single, interconnected entity, fostering a sense of shared responsibility and mutual respect. This worldview challenges divisive forces, such as regionalism, communalism, and casteism, by highlighting the common humanity that binds all Indians together. *Sarve Janaha Sukhino Bhavantu* complements this by advocating for the welfare and happiness of all, irrespective of their background. It underscores the importance of social justice, equality, and compassion in building a harmonious and unified society. By examining the historical roots, philosophical underpinnings, and contemporary relevance of these ideals, we can understand their potential to strengthen the bonds of unity within Bharat and guide the nation towards a more inclusive and prosperous future.

The historical roots of *Vasudhaiva Kutumbakam* and *Sarve Janaha Sukhino Bhavantu* can be traced back to the ancient scriptures and philosophical traditions of India. The *Maha Upanishad*, a significant text in Hindu philosophy, explicitly mentions *Vasudhaiva Kutumbakam*, encapsulating the idea that the entire world constitutes a single family. This concept is not limited to Hinduism; similar notions of universal interconnectedness and compassion are found in Jainism and Buddhism, further solidifying its place as a pan-Indian ideal. The Mauryan emperor Ashoka, a pivotal figure in Indian history, embraced these principles and propagated them through his edicts. His commitment to *dharma* (righteous conduct) and the welfare of all beings reflects the practical application of *Sarve Janaha Sukhino Bhavantu*. Ashoka's policies, focused on social justice, environmental protection, and interfaith harmony, demonstrate how these ideals can translate into concrete actions that promote unity and well-being. The Bhakti and Sufi movements of the medieval period further reinforced these values. Saints and mystics from diverse backgrounds emphasized love, devotion, and the equality of all human beings, transcending religious and social barriers. Their teachings, often expressed in vernacular languages, resonated with the masses and fostered a sense of shared identity. Figures like Kabir, Guru Nanak, and Nizamuddin Auliya championed inclusivity and challenged orthodoxies, contributing to a more syncretic and harmonious society. The emphasis on ethical conduct, social responsibility, and the recognition of the inherent dignity of every individual laid a strong foundation for a unified Bharat, rooted in shared values and a collective vision of a just and compassionate world. These historical examples illustrate the enduring relevance of these ideals in shaping the socio-political landscape of the nation.

The philosophical underpinnings of *Vasudhaiva Kutumbakam* and *Sarve Janaha Sukhino Bhavantu* are deeply rooted in the Advaita Vedanta philosophy, which posits the oneness of all existence. This non-dualistic perspective emphasizes that the individual self (*Atman*) is ultimately identical to the universal self (*Brahman*), fostering concept of *dharma* plays a crucial role in translating these ideals into practical action. *Dharma* encompasses ethical duties, righteous conduct, and the pursuit of social harmony. It emphasizes the importance of fulfilling one's responsibilities towards oneself, family, community, and the world at large. By adhering to *dharma*, individuals contribute to the overall well-being of society and promote a sense of collective purpose. The principle of *ahimsa* (non-violence) is also intrinsically linked to these ideals. *Ahimsa* extends beyond physical non-violence to encompass non-harming in thought, word, and deed. It promotes empathy, compassion, and respect for all life forms, fostering a culture of peace and understanding. Mahatma Gandhi, a staunch advocate of *ahimsa*, demonstrated its power as a tool for social and political change, inspiring movements for justice and equality around the world. These philosophical concepts provide a robust framework for building a unified Bharat, grounded in the principles of oneness, ethical conduct, and non-violence. They encourage individuals to transcend narrow self-interests and embrace a broader vision of collective well-being, fostering a society where everyone can thrive.

In contemporary Bharat, the ideals of *Vasudhaiva Kutumbakam* and *Sarve Janaha Sukhino Bhavantu* face both opportunities and challenges. Globalization has brought the world closer, making the concept of a global family more relevant than ever. Bharat's growing role on the international stage provides an opportunity to promote these ideals and advocate for a more just and equitable world order. However, internal divisions, such as religious polarization, caste discrimination, and economic inequality, continue to pose significant challenges to national unity. The rise of identity politics and divisive narratives threatens to undermine the spirit of inclusivity and mutual respect. To address these challenges, it is crucial to promote education that emphasizes the shared values and cultural heritage of Bharat. Incorporating the principles of *Vasudhaiva Kutumbakam* and *Sarve Janaha Sukhino Bhavantu* into the curriculum can help foster a sense of national identity that transcends narrow parochial loyalties. Furthermore, promoting interfaith dialogue and understanding can help bridge religious divides and foster a culture of mutual respect. Encouraging interactions and collaborations between different religious communities can help dispel misconceptions and build trust. Addressing economic inequality is also essential for promoting unity and social harmony. Ensuring access to education, healthcare, and economic opportunities for all citizens, regardless of their background, can help create a more just and equitable society. Strengthening democratic institutions and promoting good governance are also crucial for upholding the principles of *Sarve Janaha Sukhino Bhavantu*. Ensuring transparency, accountability, and the rule of law can help build trust in government and promote a sense of collective ownership. By actively promoting these ideals in education, public discourse, and policy-making, Bharat can strengthen its internal unity and project a message of peace, harmony, and universal well-being to the world. These efforts are essential for realizing the full potential of these timeless principles in the 21st century.

The practical application of *Vasudhaiva Kutumbakam* and *Sarve Janaha Sukhino Bhavantu* requires a multi-faceted approach involving individuals, communities, and the government. At the individual level, it entails cultivating empathy, compassion, and a sense of responsibility towards others. This can be fostered through practices such as volunteering, charitable giving, and engaging in acts of kindness. At the community level, it involves promoting inclusivity, social harmony, and collective action. This can be achieved through initiatives such as interfaith gatherings, community development projects, and promoting cultural exchange. The government plays a crucial role in creating an enabling environment for these ideals to flourish. This includes enacting policies that promote social justice, equality, and environmental sustainability. Investing in education, healthcare, and infrastructure can help improve the quality of life for all citizens and reduce disparities. Furthermore, the government can promote these ideals through public awareness campaigns, cultural programs, and international collaborations. By showcasing Bharat's rich cultural heritage and philosophical traditions, the government can inspire citizens to embrace these values and promote them on the global stage. Supporting civil society organizations and grassroots movements that are working to promote social change and community development is also essential. These organizations often play a vital role in reaching marginalized communities and addressing pressing social issues. Through a concerted effort involving all stakeholders, Bharat can translate these lofty ideals into tangible realities, creating a more just, equitable, and harmonious society for all. This collaborative approach is vital for ensuring that the benefits of progress reach every corner of the nation.

Looking ahead, the ideals of *Vasudhaiva Kutumbakam* and *Sarve Janaha Sukhino Bhavantu* can serve as a powerful compass guiding Bharat's future trajectory. As the world grapples with complex challenges such as climate change, pandemics, and social inequality, these principles offer a framework for building a more sustainable and equitable future. Embracing a holistic approach to development that prioritizes both economic growth and social well-being is essential. This involves investing in renewable energy, promoting sustainable agriculture, and ensuring access to clean water and sanitation for all. Strengthening social safety nets and providing support for vulnerable populations can help reduce inequality and promote social inclusion. Furthermore, promoting ethical leadership and good governance is crucial for building trust and ensuring that development benefits all segments of society. Encouraging transparency, accountability, and citizen participation can help create a more responsive and effective government. Investing in research and innovation can help Bharat develop solutions to address pressing global challenges. This includes promoting scientific advancements in areas such as healthcare, agriculture, and renewable energy. Fostering international collaborations and partnerships can help Bharat share its knowledge and expertise with the world. By actively promoting these ideals on the global stage, Bharat can play a leading role in shaping a more just and sustainable world order. This includes advocating for multilateralism, promoting peaceful conflict resolution, and working to address global challenges such as climate change and poverty. The youth of Bharat have a crucial role to play in realizing this vision. By embracing these ideals and becoming active agents of change, they can help build a brighter future for themselves and for generations to come. Their energy, creativity, and commitment are essential for translating these timeless principles into concrete action. The continued relevance and application of these ideals will shape Bharat's identity and contribution to the world.

The ideals of *Vasudhaiva kutumbakam* and *Sarve Janaha Sukhino Bhavantu* are not relics of the past but living principles that hold immense relevance for contemporary Bharat. Their enduring power lies in their ability to transcend narrow identities and foster a sense of shared humanity. By embracing these values, Bharat can strengthen its internal unity and project a message of peace, harmony, and universal well-being to the world. The journey towards realizing these ideals is an ongoing process, requiring sustained effort and commitment from individuals, communities, and the government. It demands a willingness to confront internal divisions, address social inequalities, and promote ethical conduct in all spheres of life. Education, dialogue, and collective action are essential tools for navigating this path. As Bharat continues to evolve and assert its role on the global stage, these principles can serve as a moral compass, guiding its actions and shaping its identity. By prioritizing the well-being of all and promoting a vision of interconnectedness, Bharat can contribute to a more just, sustainable, and peaceful world. The potential of these ideals to inspire positive change is immense, offering a pathway towards a future where all beings can thrive in harmony. The commitment to these principles will not only define Bharat's internal strength but also its contribution to global well-being.

India, often hailed as the world's largest democracy, stands as a vibrant tapestry woven from a multitude of cultures, languages, religions, and traditions. This inherent diversity, far As Bharat embarks on its journey towards 2047, marking a century of independence, understanding and leveraging this unity in diversity becomes paramount to realizing its full potential on the global stage. The concept transcends mere tolerance; it embodies a proactive embrace of differences, fostering an environment where varied perspectives contribute to a richer, more nuanced understanding of challenges and opportunities. It acknowledges that progress is not achieved through homogenization, but through the synergistic interaction of diverse skills, knowledge, and experiences. This introduction will explore how the principle of unity in diversity can serve as a guiding light for Bharat's trajectory towards 2047, examining its implications for socio-economic development, cultural preservation, and global leadership. It will delve into the historical context of this concept, analyze its contemporary relevance, and propose strategies for its effective implementation in shaping a future where every citizen feels empowered and included in the nation's progress.

The historical roots of unity in diversity In India are deeply embedded in its ancient civilization, characterized by the confluence of various ethnic groups, religious beliefs, and philosophical schools of thought. From the Indus Valley Civilization to the Mauryan Empire, the subcontinent has witnessed the interaction and assimilation of diverse cultures, fostering a tradition of religious tolerance and cultural exchange. The reign of Emperor Ashoka, for instance, promoted Buddhism while respecting other faiths, laying the foundation for a pluralistic society. The Mughal era further enriched this tapestry, with rulers like Akbar advocating for religious harmony through policies such as Din-i-Ilahi, an attempt to synthesize elements from different religions. However, the colonial period presented challenges to this inherent unity, as the British employed divide-

and-rule tactics to consolidate their power, exacerbating existing social divisions along religious and caste lines. Despite these challenges, the spirit of unity in diversity persisted throughout the independence movement, with leaders like Mahatma Gandhi advocating for Hindu-Muslim unity and social justice for all. The Indian Constitution, adopted in 1950, enshrined the principles of secularism, equality, and fraternity, aiming to create a just and inclusive society that respects the rights and freedoms of all its citizens. Article 14 guarantees equality before the law, while Articles 15 and 16 prohibit discrimination on the grounds of religion, race, caste, sex, or place of birth. Furthermore, the Constitution recognizes the rights of linguistic and religious minorities, ensuring their representation and participation in the political process. The concept of unity in diversity is not merely a historical artifact but a living reality that continues to shape India's identity and trajectory. It is reflected in the country's vibrant cultural landscape, where diverse art forms, music, dance, and literature coexist and enrich each other. From the classical traditions of Bharatanatyam and Kathak to the folk dances of various regions, India's cultural heritage is a testament to its pluralistic ethos. Similarly, the country's linguistic diversity, with over 22 officially recognized languages and hundreds of dialects, reflects its rich cultural mosaic. This historical foundation provides a crucial context for understanding the contemporary challenges and opportunities facing Bharat as it strives to achieve its aspirations for 2047. The ability to draw.

In the contemporary context, unity in diversity plays a crucial role in fostering socio-economic development and inclusive growth in Bharat. Recognizing and celebrating diversity can unlock a wealth of human potential, driving innovation, creativity, and entrepreneurship. A diverse workforce, for instance, brings a variety of perspectives and experiences to the table, leading to more effective problem-solving and decision-making. Studies have shown that companies with diverse leadership teams are more likely to outperform their less diverse counterparts. Furthermore, embracing diversity can enhance social cohesion and reduce inequality, creating a more just and equitable society. By promoting equal opportunities for all, regardless of their background, Bharat can tap into the talents and skills of its entire population, accelerating economic progress and improving the quality of life for all its citizens. However, realizing the benefits of unity in diversity requires proactive policies and initiatives to address historical injustices and systemic inequalities. This includes affirmative action programs to promote the representation of marginalized communities in education and employment, as well as measures to combat discrimination and prejudice. Investing in education and skills development is also essential to empower individuals from diverse backgrounds to participate fully in the economy and society. Moreover, promoting intercultural dialogue and understanding can help to bridge divides and foster a sense of shared citizenship. By creating spaces for people from different backgrounds to interact and learn from each other, Bharat can build a more inclusive and harmonious society. The effective management of diversity is not merely a social imperative but also an economic necessity for Bharat's continued progress and prosperity.

Looking ahead to 2047, unity in diversity will be instrumental in shaping Bharat's role as a global leader. In an increasingly interconnected world, the ability to understand and engage with different cultures and perspectives is essential for effective diplomacy, trade, and international cooperation. Bharat's unique experience in managing diversity within its own borders can serve as a valuable model for other nations grappling with similar challenges. By promoting its pluralistic ethos and advocating for inclusive governance on the global stage, Bharat can enhance its soft power and strengthen its relationships with countries around the world. Furthermore, embracing diversity can foster innovation and creativity, enabling Bharat to become a hub for cutting-edge research and development. By attracting talent from diverse backgrounds and creating an environment that encourages collaboration and experimentation, Bharat can drive technological advancements and address pressing global challenges such as climate change, poverty, and disease. However, realizing this vision requires a concerted effort to promote intercultural understanding and global citizenship among its citizens. This includes incorporating global perspectives into the education curriculum, encouraging student exchange programs, and supporting initiatives that promote cross-cultural dialogue and collaboration. Moreover, Bharat must continue to uphold its commitment to human rights and democratic values, serving as a beacon of hope and inspiration for countries striving for greater freedom and equality. By embracing its diversity and promoting inclusivity, Bharat can emerge as a global leader that champions peace, prosperity, and sustainability for all. The nation's ability to harness its internal diversity will directly influence its capacity to navigate the complexities of the international arena and contribute meaningfully to global solutions.

Despite the potential benefits, realizing unity in diversity in Bharat faces several challenges that need to be addressed proactively. One of the main challenges is the persistence of social inequalities based on caste, religion, gender, and region. These inequalities can lead to discrimination, marginalization, and social unrest, undermining the fabric of unity and hindering inclusive growth. Addressing these inequalities requires a multi-pronged approach that includes affirmative action, targeted social programs, and legal reforms to ensure equal opportunities for all. Another challenge is the rise of divisive ideologies and hate speech, which can polarize society and erode trust between different communities. The spread of misinformation and disinformation through social media can further exacerbate these divisions, making it difficult to promote dialogue and understanding. Combating hate speech and promoting media literacy are essential to safeguard the values of unity and tolerance. Furthermore, the increasing pressure on natural resources and the impacts of climate change can exacerbate existing social tensions, particularly in marginalized communities that are disproportionately affected by environmental degradation. Addressing climate change and promoting sustainable development are crucial to ensure that all citizens have access to basic necessities and opportunities for a better life. Moreover, the lack of effective governance and accountability can undermine public trust and erode the legitimacy of state institutions. Strengthening governance, promoting transparency, and ensuring the rule of law are essential to create a level playing field and foster a sense of shared citizenship. Overcoming these challenges requires a collective effort from government, civil society, and individuals to promote inclusivity, justice, and equality for all. The success of Bharat's journey towards 2047 hinges on its ability to address these challenges and harness the full potential of its diverse population.

To effectively move ahead with unity in diversity as a guiding principle for Bharat at 2047, several key strategies need to be implemented. Firstly, education plays a vital role in fostering intercultural understanding and promoting tolerance. The curriculum should be designed to reflect the diversity of India's cultural heritage, incorporating the histories, languages, and traditions of different communities. Promoting critical thinking and media literacy can also help students to discern fact from fiction and resist divisive ideologies. Secondly, promoting inclusive governance and participatory democracy is essential to ensure that all citizens have a voice in shaping the future of the nation. This includes strengthening local governance, empowering marginalized communities, and promoting transparency and accountability in public institutions. Creating platforms for dialogue and consultation between government, civil society, and citizens can also help to build trust and foster a sense of shared ownership. Thirdly, investing in social programs that address inequality and promote social justice is crucial to ensure that all citizens have access to basic necessities and opportunities for a better life. This includes providing quality education, healthcare, and affordable housing, as well as promoting employment and entrepreneurship. Targeted programs should be designed to address the specific needs of marginalized communities, such as women, minorities, and persons with disabilities. Fourthly, promoting cultural exchange and artistic expression can help to bridge divides and foster a sense of shared identity. Supporting cultural festivals, art exhibitions, and literary events that showcase the diversity of India's cultural heritage can create spaces for people from different backgrounds to interact and learn from each other. These strategies, implemented comprehensively, will pave the way for a more unified and prosperous Bharat by 2047.

As Bharat journeys towards 2047, the principle of unity in diversity stands as a cornerstone for its future success and global leadership. Embracing this concept requires a conscious and sustained effort to address historical inequalities, promote inclusive governance, and foster intercultural understanding. The challenges are significant, ranging from persistent social divisions to the rise of divisive ideologies, but the potential rewards are immense. A Bharat that truly embodies unity in diversity will be a nation where every citizen feels valued, empowered, and included in the nation's progress. This will not only enhance social cohesion and stability but also unlock the full potential of its human capital, driving innovation, creativity, and economic growth. Furthermore, a Bharat that champions unity in diversity will be well-positioned to play a leading role on the global stage, promoting peace, prosperity, and sustainability for all. Its unique experience in managing diversity within its own borders can serve as a valuable model for other nations grappling with similar challenges. However, realizing this vision requires a collective commitment from government, civil society, and individuals to uphold the values of justice, equality, and fraternity. It requires a willingness to engage in open and honest dialogue, to challenge prejudice and discrimination, and to work together to build a more inclusive and harmonious society. The path towards 2047 will undoubtedly be filled with challenges and uncertainties, but by staying true to the principles of unity in diversity, Bharat can overcome these obstacles and emerge as a truly great nation, a beacon of hope and inspiration for the world. The strength of Bharat lies not in its uniformity, but in its vibrant tapestry of cultures, languages, and traditions, woven together by a shared commitment.

Swami Vivekananda, a towering figure in the modern Indian renaissance, envisioned a world bound by the threads of universal brotherhood, a concept deeply rooted in the ancient Vedantic philosophy. His message resonated powerfully during a time of burgeoning nationalism and increasing global interconnectedness, offering a unique perspective on how humanity could navigate the complexities of cultural and religious differences. Vivekananda's advocacy for universal brotherhood wasn't merely a utopian ideal; it was a pragmatic approach to fostering unity amidst the inherent diversity of the human experience. His teachings emphasized the inherent divinity within each individual, transcending the superficial barriers of caste, creed, nationality, and religion. This core belief formed the bedrock of his call for a global community where mutual respect, understanding, and empathy would prevail. Vivekananda believed that recognizing the shared spiritual essence of all beings was the key to overcoming prejudice, conflict, and the divisive forces that plagued society. The concept of unity in diversity, central to Vivekananda's philosophy, acknowledges and celebrates the richness and variety of human cultures and beliefs, while simultaneously emphasizing the underlying unity that binds us together. He argued that true unity doesn't necessitate uniformity; rather, it thrives on the harmonious coexistence of diverse perspectives and traditions. Vivekananda's vision offers a compelling framework for addressing contemporary challenges related to globalization, cultural integration, and the rise of identity politics, providing a timeless message of hope and a pathway towards a more inclusive and peaceful world.

The philosophical foundation of Vivekananda's concept of universal brotherhood lies in Advaita Vedanta, a school of Hindu philosophy that posits the ultimate reality as Brahman, the one, indivisible, and all-pervading consciousness. This philosophy asserts that every individual soul (Atman) is essentially identical to Brahman, implying a fundamental unity underlying all apparent differences. Vivekananda masterfully translated this complex metaphysical concept into a practical ethical framework, arguing that recognizing the inherent divinity within oneself naturally leads to recognizing it in others. This realization, he believed, would dismantle the ego-driven barriers that separate individuals and foster a sense of interconnectedness and empathy. Vivekananda's interpretation of Vedanta emphasized its social implications, moving beyond purely individualistic spiritual pursuits. He saw the practical application of Vedanta as a means to alleviate suffering, promote social justice, and bridge the divides between different communities. He vehemently criticized the rigid caste system prevalent in India, arguing that it contradicted the Vedantic principle of the inherent equality of all beings. His advocacy for the upliftment of the marginalized and oppressed stemmed directly from his belief in the universal brotherhood, urging individuals to see beyond superficial differences and recognize the shared humanity of all. Furthermore, Vivekananda's understanding of Vedanta extended beyond the confines of Hinduism, recognizing the common threads of spiritual wisdom that run through various religious traditions. He believed that each religion, in its purest form, offered a unique path to realizing the same ultimate truth, advocating for interfaith dialogue and mutual respect as essential components of universal brotherhood. This inclusive approach distinguished him from narrow-minded religious dogmatism and positioned him as a champion of religious harmony and understanding, demonstrating the profound impact of Vedantic philosophy on his vision of a unified world.

Vivekananda's articulation of universal brotherhood extended beyond mere philosophical discourse; he actively promoted its practical application through his teachings and actions. His famous address at the Parliament of the World's Religions in Chicago in 1893 served as a pivotal moment in disseminating his message to a global audience. There, he eloquently presented Hinduism not as a collection of dogmas, but as a philosophy of universalism, tolerance, and acceptance. He emphasized the common ground shared by all religions, advocating for an end to religious fanaticism and sectarianism. His powerful words resonated deeply with listeners, challenging prevailing Western perceptions of Eastern spirituality and paving the way for greater interfaith understanding. Following his success in Chicago, Vivekananda embarked on extensive travels across the United States and Europe, establishing Vedanta Societies and delivering lectures on various aspects of Indian philosophy and culture. These efforts were instrumental in fostering cross-cultural dialogue and promoting a more nuanced understanding of Eastern traditions. He consistently emphasized the importance of education, service to humanity, and the cultivation of moral character as essential components of realizing universal brotherhood. Vivekananda's emphasis on practical Vedanta also manifested in his focus on social reform within India. He established the Ramakrishna Mission, an organization dedicated to serving the poor and needy, providing education, healthcare, and disaster relief. This commitment to social service demonstrated his belief that spiritual realization must be accompanied by concrete action to alleviate suffering and promote the well-being of all. Through his tireless efforts, Vivekananda demonstrated that universal brotherhood was not merely an abstract ideal, but a tangible goal that could be achieved through education, interfaith dialogue, and selfless service. His life exemplified the transformative power of embracing the interconnectedness of humanity and working towards a more just and compassionate world.

The concept of unity in diversity, as championed by Vivekananda, offers a particularly relevant framework for navigating the complexities of the modern world, characterized by increasing globalization and the rise of multicultural societies. In an era marked by both unprecedented interconnectedness and heightened social divisions, Vivekananda's message provides a pathway towards fostering harmonious coexistence and mutual understanding. He recognized that true unity does not require the suppression of individual identities or cultural differences; rather, it thrives on the celebration and appreciation of the richness and variety of human expression. Vivekananda's vision challenges the notion that diversity is inherently a source of conflict, arguing instead that it can be a source of strength and innovation. By embracing different perspectives and learning from diverse cultures, societies can become more resilient, adaptable, and creative. His emphasis on recognizing the underlying unity of all beings serves as a powerful antidote to the divisive forces of prejudice, discrimination, and xenophobia. Furthermore, Vivekananda's teachings offer valuable insights for addressing contemporary challenges related to identity politics and the rise of nationalism. He cautioned against the dangers of narrow-minded nationalism, which can lead to exclusion, conflict, and the denial of universal human rights. Instead, he advocated for a form of patriotism that is rooted in a sense of global citizenship and a commitment to the well-being of all humanity. His message encourages individuals to embrace their national identities while simultaneously recognizing their shared responsibility to the global community. Vivekananda's concept of unity in diversity provides a timeless message of hope and a practical framework for building a more inclusive, peaceful, and prosperous world for all. His teachings continue to inspire individuals and communities to bridge divides, overcome prejudice, and work towards a future where the inherent dignity and worth of every human being is respected and celebrated.

Despite the enduring relevance of Vivekananda's message, its implementation faces significant challenges in a world grappling with persistent inequalities, political polarization, and environmental degradation. The gap between the ideal of universal brotherhood and the realities of global power dynamics remains vast, requiring sustained effort and critical self-reflection. One of the key challenges lies in overcoming deeply ingrained prejudices and biases that perpetuate discrimination and inequality. These biases often operate at both conscious and unconscious levels, shaping our perceptions and interactions with others. Addressing these requires a concerted effort to promote education, awareness, and empathy, fostering a culture of inclusivity and respect for diversity. Another challenge stems from the unequal distribution of resources and opportunities across the globe. Economic disparities, political instability, and environmental degradation disproportionately affect marginalized communities, hindering their ability to participate fully in the global community. Overcoming these inequalities requires a commitment to social justice, sustainable development, and equitable access to resources. Furthermore, the rise of populism and nationalism in many parts of the world poses a threat for humanity to transcend its divisions and work towards a more just and compassionate world. However, realizing this vision requires a sustained commitment to addressing the systemic challenges that perpetuate inequality and division, demanding continuous effort to bridge the gap between the ideal and the reality.

To effectively realize Vivekananda's vision of universal brotherhood in the 21st century, a multi-faceted approach is required, encompassing individual transformation, social reform, and global cooperation. At the individual level, cultivating empathy, compassion, and a willingness to understand different perspectives is crucial. This involves actively challenging our own biases, engaging in meaningful dialogue with people from diverse backgrounds, and seeking opportunities to learn about different cultures and traditions. Education plays a vital role in fostering these qualities, promoting critical thinking, and encouraging a sense of global citizenship. Social reform is equally essential, addressing systemic inequalities and promoting social justice. This includes advocating for policies that ensure equal access to education, healthcare, and economic opportunities, as well as challenging discriminatory practices and promoting inclusivity in all spheres of life. Civil society organizations, community groups, and social movements play a critical role in driving these reforms, holding governments and corporations accountable and advocating for the rights of marginalized communities. Global cooperation is indispensable for addressing transnational challenges such as climate change, poverty, and conflict. This requires strengthening international institutions, promoting multilateralism, and fostering a sense of shared responsibility for the well-being of the planet and its inhabitants. International agreements and collaborations are essential for addressing these challenges effectively, ensuring that all countries have a voice in shaping global policies. Furthermore, technology can play a significant role in promoting universal brotherhood by connecting people across borders, facilitating cross-cultural exchange, and providing access to information and education. However, it is crucial to address the digital divide and ensure that technology is used in a way that promotes inclusivity and equity, rather than exacerbating existing inequalities. Ultimately, realizing Vivekananda's vision requires a collective effort, involving individuals, communities, governments, and international organizations working together to build a more just, peaceful, and sustainable world. It demands a shift in consciousness, from a focus on self-interest to a recognition of our interconnectedness and shared responsibility for the well-being of all humanity. By embracing Vivekananda's teachings and actively.

Swami Vivekananda's profound articulation of universal brotherhood and unity in diversity remains a beacon of hope in an increasingly complex and interconnected world. His philosophical grounding in Advaita Vedanta, coupled with his practical approach to social reform and interfaith dialogue, offers a timeless framework for navigating the challenges of cultural differences, social inequalities, and global conflict. Vivekananda's message transcends the boundaries of religion, nationality, and ideology, appealing to the shared humanity that binds us together. His emphasis on recognizing the inherent divinity within each individual serves as a powerful antidote to prejudice, discrimination, and the divisive forces that threaten to tear societies apart. His vision of unity in diversity celebrates the richness and variety of human cultures and beliefs, while simultaneously emphasizing the underlying unity that connects us all. While the path towards realizing universal brotherhood is fraught with challenges, Vivekananda's teachings provide a roadmap for building a more just, peaceful, and sustainable world. By cultivating empathy, promoting social justice, fostering global cooperation, and embracing the transformative power of education, we can strive to create a future where the inherent dignity and worth of every human being is respected and celebrated. Vivekananda's legacy continues to inspire individuals and communities around the world to bridge divides, overcome prejudice, and work towards a future where the ideal of universal brotherhood becomes a lived reality. His message serves as a constant reminder of our shared responsibility to create a world where all can thrive in peace and harmony.

The encapsulates a profound understanding of interconnectedness, emphasizing the shared humanity that binds individuals, communities, and nations together, transcending geographical, cultural, and ideological boundaries. This philosophy, rooted in the rich tapestry of Indian thought, offers a powerful framework for fostering unity in diversity, promoting peaceful coexistence, and addressing global issues through collective action. Vasudhaiva Kutumbakam is not merely a utopian ideal, but a pragmatic approach to navigating an increasingly complex and interdependent world. In an era marked by globalization, migration, and technological advancements, the lines between nations and cultures are becoming increasingly blurred. This interconnectedness presents both opportunities and challenges. While it facilitates the exchange of ideas, knowledge, and resources, it also creates new avenues for conflict, inequality, and environmental degradation. The Santana Kutumbakam, as an extension of this core philosophy, emphasizes the importance of cultivating a sense of belonging and shared responsibility within this global family. It calls for empathy, understanding, and mutual respect, urging individuals and institutions to work together to create a more just, equitable, and sustainable world for all

The historical roots of Vasudhaiva Kutumbakam can be traced back to ancient Indian scriptures, particularly the Upanishads and the Puranas. These texts articulate a worldview that emphasizes the interconnectedness of all beings and the inherent unity underlying the diversity of the manifest world. The concept is prominently featured in the Maha Upanishad, where it is stated,ending narrow self-interests and embracing a broader sense of kinship with all of humanity. The influence of Vasudhaiva Kutumbakam extends beyond religious and philosophical texts, permeating various aspects of Indian culture and social life. The emphasis on community, cooperation, and collective responsibility is deeply ingrained in traditional Indian societies, where families, villages, and communities often function as interdependent units. This spirit of collaboration and mutual support is reflected in various social practices, such as joint family systems, community-based resource management, and collective celebrations of festivals and rituals. Furthermore, the principles of Vasudhaiva Kutumbakam have also inspired numerous social and political movements in India, advocating for inclusivity, social justice, and peaceful coexistence. Leaders like Mahatma Gandhi, who championed the cause of non-violence and interfaith harmony, drew heavily from the philosophy of Vasudhaiva Kutumbakam in their struggle for independence and social reform. Gandhi's emphasis on Sarvodaya, or the welfare of all, reflected the core values of Vasudhaiva Kutumbakam, promoting a vision of society where the needs of all individuals are met and where everyone has the opportunity to thrive. The enduring relevance of Vasudhaiva Kutumbakam lies in its ability to provide a moral compass for navigating the challenges of a globalized world, fostering a sense of shared responsibility and promoting collective action to address pressing issues such as poverty, inequality, and environmental degradation. The historical and cultural context of Vasudhaiva Kutumbakam provides a foundation for understanding its significance as a guiding principle for promoting unity in diversity and building a more just and sustainable world.

The philosophical underpinnings of Vasudhaiva Kutumbakam rest on the Advaita Vedanta school of thought, which posits the non-duality of reality, asserting that all beings are interconnected and ultimately part of the same universal consciousness. This perspective challenges the notion of separateness and emphasizes the inherent unity underlying the diversity of the manifest world. From an Advaita Vedanta perspective, the perception of difference and division is an illusion, born out of ignorance and attachment to the ego. By recognizing the underlying unity of all beings, individuals can transcend their limited self-identity and cultivate a sense of empathy, compassion, and interconnectedness with others. This philosophical framework provides a powerful basis for promoting inclusivity, tolerance, and mutual respect, fostering a sense of belonging and shared responsibility within the global community. Furthermore, the philosophy of Vasudhaiva Kutumbakam aligns with ethical principles such as Ahimsa (non-violence), Satya (truthfulness), and Dharma (righteous conduct), which emphasize the importance of treating all beings with respect and compassion. These ethical guidelines provide a practical framework for translating the philosophical ideals of Vasudhaiva Kutumbakam into concrete actions, promoting peaceful coexistence, social justice, and environmental sustainability. The philosophical depth of Vasudhaiva Kutumbakam offers a profound understanding of interconnectedness, providing a strong foundation for fostering unity in diversity and addressing global challenges through collective action.

The practical applications of Vasudhaiva Kutumbakam extend across various spheres of human endeavor, offering a framework for promoting unity in diversity and addressing global challenges through collective action. In the realm of international relations, the philosophy of Vasudhaiva Kutumbakam can serve as a guiding principle for fostering peaceful coexistence, promoting diplomacy, and resolving conflicts through dialogue and negotiation. By recognizing the shared interests and common humanity of all nations, leaders can transcend narrow self-interests and work together to address global issues such as climate change, poverty, and terrorism. The concept of Vasudhaiva Kutumbakam can also inform approaches to global governance, advocating for inclusive and participatory decision-making processes that take into account the perspectives and needs of all stakeholders. In the field of economic development, the principles of Vasudhaiva Kutumbakam can promote equitable and sustainable growth, emphasizing the importance of social justice, environmental protection, and inclusive economic policies. By recognizing the interconnectedness of economic systems and the shared responsibility for the well-being of all, policymakers can prioritize investments in education, healthcare, and infrastructure, creating opportunities for all individuals to thrive. The philosophy of Vasudhaiva Kutumbakam can also inspire innovative approaches to poverty reduction, promoting community-based development initiatives that empower local communities and foster self-reliance. Furthermore, in the realm of cultural exchange and education, the principles of Vasudhaiva Kutumbakam can promote intercultural understanding, tolerance, and respect for diversity. By fostering opportunities for people from different backgrounds to interact, learn from each other, and share their experiences, societies can break down stereotypes, challenge prejudices, and build bridges of understanding. The philosophy of Vasudhaiva Kutumbakam can also inform educational curricula, promoting global citizenship education that equips students with the knowledge, skills, and values necessary to navigate an increasingly interconnected world. The diverse applications of Vasudhaiva Kutumbakam demonstrate its potential as a powerful tool for promoting unity in diversity and building a more just, equitable, and sustainable world for all.

Despite its inherent strengths, the application of Vasudhaiva Kutumbakam also faces certain challenges and criticisms. One of the main challenges lies in reconciling the ideal of universal unity with the realities of power politics, national interests, and cultural differences. In a world characterized by competing interests and conflicting ideologies, it can be difficult to translate the principles of Vasudhaiva Kutumbakam into concrete actions that promote cooperation and mutual understanding. Critics also argue that the concept of Vasudhaiva Kutumbakam can be interpreted in different ways, leading to divergent approaches and potentially conflicting outcomes. Some may view it as a call for global homogenization, while others may emphasize the importance of preserving cultural diversity and respecting national sovereignty. Furthermore, the implementation of Vasudhaiva Kutumbakam requires a fundamental shift in mindset, moving away from narrow self-interests and embracing a broader sense of shared responsibility. This can be a difficult process, particularly in societies where individualism, competition, and material gain are highly valued. Overcoming these challenges requires a concerted effort to promote dialogue, build trust, and foster a shared understanding of the principles and values underlying Vasudhaiva Kutumbakam. Addressing these challenges is crucial for realizing the full potential of Vasudhaiva Kutumbakam as a guiding principle for promoting unity in diversity and building a more peaceful and sustainable world.

To effectively leverage Vasudhaiva Kutumbakam in today's world, several strategies can be adopted. Firstly, promoting education and awareness about the philosophy and its practical applications is crucial. This can be achieved through integrating the principles of Vasudhaiva Kutumbakam into educational curricula at all levels, organizing workshops and seminars, and utilizing media platforms to disseminate information and promote dialogue. Secondly, fostering intercultural understanding and exchange is essential for building bridges of trust and breaking down stereotypes. This can involve supporting cultural exchange programs, promoting language learning, and encouraging people from different backgrounds to interact and learn from each other. Thirdly, strengthening international cooperation and global governance mechanisms is necessary for addressing shared challenges and promoting collective action. This can entail supporting multilateral institutions, promoting diplomacy and negotiation, and advocating for inclusive and participatory decision-making processes. Fourthly, promoting ethical leadership and responsible citizenship is vital for translating the principles of Vasudhaiva Kutumbakam into concrete actions. This can involve fostering a culture of integrity, accountability, and transparency in all spheres of life, and encouraging individuals to take responsibility for their actions and contribute to the well-being of their communities. Fifthly, leveraging technology and innovation can help to connect people across borders, facilitate communication, and promote collaboration. This can involve utilizing social media platforms to share information, organize campaigns, and mobilize support for various causes, and developing innovative solutions to address global challenges such as climate change, poverty, and disease. By implementing these strategies, societies can harness the transformative potential of Vasudhaiva Kutumbakam to build a more just, equitable, and sustainable world for all, fostering a sense of shared responsibility and promoting collective action to address pressing global issues. These multifaceted approaches are vital for realizing the full potential of Vasudhaiva Kutumbakam in the contemporary global landscape.

The Santana Kutumbakam offers a powerful framework for navigating the complexities of an increasingly interconnected world, promoting unity in diversity and fostering a sense of shared responsibility for the well-being of all. Rooted in ancient Indian philosophy and culture, this concept emphasizes the interconnectedness of all beings and the inherent unity underlying the diversity of the manifest world. While the application of Vasudhaiva Kutumbakam faces certain challenges, its potential as a guiding principle for promoting peaceful coexistence, social justice, and environmental sustainability remains immense. By promoting education and awareness, fostering intercultural understanding, strengthening international cooperation, promoting ethical leadership, and leveraging technology and innovation, societies can harness the transformative power of Vasudhaiva Kutumbakam to build a more just, equitable, and sustainable world for all.The enduring relevance of Vasudhaiva Kutumbakam lies in its ability to provide a moral compass for navigating the challenges of globalization, fostering a sense of shared humanity, and promoting collective action to address pressing global issues. As the world becomes increasingly interconnected, the need for a philosophy that emphasizes unity in diversity and promotes cooperation among nations and cultures becomes ever more urgent. The Santana Kutumbakam offers a timeless message of hope and a practical framework for building a better future for all, inspiring individuals and institutions to work together to create a world where everyone can thrive.

Bharat This concept, far from being a modern political slogan, is deeply rooted in the historical development of the region, particularly during ancient times. The Indian subcontinent, a melting pot of diverse ethnicities, languages, religions, and cultures, presents a compelling case study of how a shared sense of identity and collective purpose can emerge and flourish amidst profound differences.The glory of ancient Bharat lies not just in its magnificent empires, philosophical advancements, or artistic achievements, but also in its unique ability to weave together a tapestry of disparate elements into a cohesive whole. From the Indus Valley Civilization to the Mauryan Empire, and through the subsequent rise of various kingdoms and dynasties, the narrative of ancient India is one of continuous interaction, assimilation, and adaptation. This historical process provides a leading example of how a society can embrace and celebrate its internal variations while simultaneously forging a strong and unified national character. Understanding this historical development is crucial for appreciating the enduring strength and resilience of India's cultural fabric and its continued relevance in the modern world. The ancient period laid the foundation for many of the social, political, and cultural norms that continue to shape India today, making it a fascinating and instructive example for other diverse societies around the globe.

The Indus Valley Civilization (IVC), flourishing from around 3300 to 1700 BCE, provides an early glimpse into the dynamics of unity in diversity in the Indian subcontinent. Archaeological evidence suggests a remarkable degree of standardization in urban planning, weights and measures, and even script across a vast geographical area encompassing modern-day Pakistan and northwest India. This uniformity hints at a centralized authority or a network of interconnected urban centers that facilitated trade, communication, and cultural exchange.

However, the IVC was not monolithic. Different settlements exhibited variations in pottery styles, burial practices, and other cultural artifacts, indicating the presence of distinct regional identities within a broader framework of shared civilization. The presence of diverse occupational groups, including farmers, artisans, traders, and priests, further underscores the social complexity of the IVC. The civilization's sophisticated water management systems, including wells, reservoirs, and drainage networks, demonstrate a collective effort to harness natural resources and adapt to the environment. This collaborative spirit likely extended to other aspects of life, fostering a sense of shared responsibility and mutual dependence among the inhabitants of the IVC. The decline of the IVC around 1700 BCE marked a period of transition and upheaval in the Indian subcontinent. The subsequent arrival of Indo-Aryan-speaking groups from Central Asia led to a fusion of cultures and the emergence of new social and political formations. The Vedic period, spanning from around 1500 to 500 BCE, witnessed the composition of the Vedas, a collection of sacred texts that laid the foundation for Hinduism. The Vedic texts reflect a society characterized by a hierarchical social structure, with priests (Brahmins), warriors (Kshatriyas), merchants (Vaishyas), and laborers (Shudras) occupying distinct positions in the social order. However, the Vedic period also saw the rise of dissenting voices and alternative philosophical schools, such as the Upanishads, which challenged the rigid social hierarchy and emphasized the importance of individual spiritual experience. This intellectual ferment contributed to the development of a pluralistic and tolerant intellectual climate, where different viewpoints could coexist and even enrich one another. The seeds of unity in diversity were sown in the very foundations of ancient Indian society, setting the stage for the subsequent development of a complex and multifaceted civilization.

The Mauryan Empire (322-185 BCE), founded by Chandragupta Maurya, represents a significant milestone in the political unification of the Indian subcontinent. Ashoka, the third Mauryan emperor, played a pivotal role in promoting unity and harmony through his policy of Dhamma, which emphasized non-violence, tolerance, and social welfare. Ashoka's edicts, inscribed on pillars and rocks throughout the empire, promoted ethical conduct, respect for all religions, and compassion for all living beings. These edicts, written in various local languages, demonstrate Ashoka's commitment to communicating with his diverse subjects in their own tongues. The Mauryan Empire's vast administrative network, with its centralized bureaucracy and standardized legal system, facilitated trade, communication, and cultural exchange across different regions. However, the empire also recognized and respected local customs and traditions, allowing for a degree of regional autonomy within a broader framework of imperial unity. The Mauryan period witnessed the flourishing of various religious and philosophical traditions, including Buddhism, Jainism, and Hinduism. Ashoka's patronage of Buddhism contributed to its spread throughout the Indian subcontinent and beyond, but he also supported other religious sects and encouraged interfaith dialogue. This policy of religious tolerance fostered a climate of peaceful coexistence and mutual respect among different religious communities. The Mauryan Empire's economic prosperity, fueled by agriculture, trade, and manufacturing, contributed to the growth of urban centers and the development of a vibrant mercantile class. The empire's extensive road network, including the Grand Trunk Road, facilitated the movement of goods and people, connecting different regions and promoting economic integration. The Mauryan Empire's legacy of political unity, religious tolerance, and social welfare continued to influence subsequent rulers and dynasties in the Indian subcontinent, shaping the course of Indian history for centuries to come. The empire's ability to reconcile centralized authority with regional diversity provides a valuable lesson in governance and nation-building.

Following the decline of the Mauryan Empire, the Indian subcontinent witnessed the rise of numerous regional kingdoms and empires, each with its own distinct cultural and political identity. The cultural flourishing. The Gupta rulers promoted Hinduism and patronized Sanskrit literature, art, and science. However, they also maintained a policy of religious tolerance, allowing Buddhism and Jainism to thrive alongside Hinduism. The Gupta period saw the development of a sophisticated legal system, based on the principles of Dharma, Artha, and Kama.

The Gupta rulers also promoted trade and commerce, fostering economic prosperity and cultural exchange with other parts of the world. The Gupta Empire's cultural achievements, including the development of the decimal system, the invention of chess, and the creation of masterpieces of Sanskrit literature, had a lasting impact on Indian civilization. The period also saw the rise of regional languages and literatures, reflecting the growing cultural diversity of the Indian subcontinent. The subsequent centuries witnessed the emergence of various regional powers, including the Pallavas, Chalukyas, and Rashtrakutas in the south, and the Rajputs and Palas in the north. These kingdoms often engaged in warfare with one another, but they also fostered cultural exchange and economic cooperation. The rise of these regional powers contributed to the development of a complex and multifaceted cultural landscape, characterized by a rich tapestry of languages, religions, and artistic traditions. The ability of different kingdoms and cultures to coexist and interact with one another demonstrates the enduring strength of India's tradition of unity in diversity.

The religious landscape of ancient India was characterized by a remarkable degree of diversity and tolerance. Hinduism, with its diverse pantheon of gods and goddesses, its emphasis on dharma and karma, and its various philosophical schools, provided a broad framework for spiritual expression. Buddhism, founded by Siddhartha Gautama, offered an alternative path to enlightenment, emphasizing non-violence, compassion, and the Four Noble Truths. Jainism, with its emphasis on ahimsa (non-violence) and asceticism, also attracted a significant following. These three major religions coexisted and interacted with one another, influencing each other's doctrines and practices. The concept of religious tolerance was deeply ingrained in ancient Indian society. Rulers often patronized multiple religions, and interfaith dialogue was common. The Ashokan edicts, for example, emphasized the importance of respecting all religions and avoiding sectarian conflict. The Bhagavad Gita, a central text of Hinduism, advocates for the acceptance of different paths to God. The rise of Bhakti movements, which emphasized personal devotion to a particular deity, further contributed to the diversification of religious expression. These movements often transcended caste and class barriers, attracting followers from all sections of society. The construction of temples, monasteries, and stupas dedicated to different deities and religious figures reflected the religious pluralism of ancient India. These religious structures served as centers of learning, art, and culture, contributing to the overall richness and diversity of Indian civilization. The interaction between different religions also led to the development of syncretic traditions, which combined elements of different faiths. For example, some Hindu deities were incorporated into Buddhist pantheons, and vice versa. The religious diversity of ancient India was not without its challenges. There were occasional instances of religious conflict and persecution. However, the overall trend was towards tolerance and coexistence. The ability of different religions to coexist and interact with one another demonstrates the enduring strength of India's tradition of unity in diversity. The religious landscape of ancient.

The economic prosperity of ancient Bharat was driven by a combination of agriculture, trade, and manufacturing. The fertile river valleys of the Indus, Ganges, and Brahmaputra supported a thriving agricultural sector, producing a variety of crops, including rice, wheat, barley, and cotton. Trade flourished both within the Indian subcontinent and with other parts of the world, including Mesopotamia, Egypt, and Southeast Asia. Indian merchants exported textiles, spices, precious stones, and other goods, and imported gold, silver, and horses. The development of coinage facilitated trade and commerce, and the establishment of trade routes connected different regions and cultures. Manufacturing also played a significant role in the ancient Indian economy. Indian artisans produced a wide range of goods, including pottery, textiles, metalwork, and jewelry. The quality of Indian craftsmanship was renowned throughout the ancient world. The caste system, while often criticized for its social inequalities, also played a role in the organization of the economy. Different castes were traditionally associated with different occupations, and this division of labor contributed to the efficiency of the economy. The economic prosperity of ancient Bharat supported the growth of urban centers and the development of a vibrant mercantile class. Cities such as Taxila, Pataliputra, and Madurai served as centers of trade, culture, and learning. The economic interactions between different regions and cultures contributed to the diffusion of ideas and technologies. The economic dynamism of ancient India demonstrates the importance of diversity and interconnectedness in fostering prosperity. The ability of different regions and communities to specialize in different economic activities and to trade with one another contributed to the overall wealth and well-being of the subcontinent.

The historical development of unity in diversity in ancient Bharat offers a compelling example of how a society can thrive amidst profound differences. From the Indus Valley Civilization to the rise of various empires and kingdoms, the Indian subcontinent has consistently demonstrated an ability to integrate diverse cultures, religions, and ethnicities into a cohesive whole. The Mauryan Empire, with its emphasis on religious tolerance and social welfare, stands as a testament to the power of inclusive governance. The Gupta period, with its flourishing of art, literature, and science, showcases the creative potential of a diverse and vibrant society. The religious landscape of ancient India, characterized by the coexistence of Hinduism, Buddhism, Jainism, and other faiths, exemplifies the importance of respecting different spiritual paths. The economic prosperity of ancient Bharat, driven by agriculture, trade, and manufacturing, highlights the benefits of interconnectedness and specialization. The legacy of ancient India continues to resonate in the modern world. The principles of religious tolerance, social justice, and inclusive governance remain relevant in an increasingly globalized and interconnected world. The challenges faced by ancient Indian societies in managing diversity and promoting unity offer valuable lessons for contemporary policymakers and community leaders. The study of ancient Bharat provides insights into the complex dynamics of cultural interaction, social cohesion, and political integration. The historical development of unity in diversity in ancient Bharat serves as an inspiration for building a more just, equitable, and harmonious world. The enduring legacy of ancient India reminds us that diversity is not a weakness but a strength, and that unity can be achieved without sacrificing individuality or cultural identity. The story of ancient

Bharat is a story of resilience, adaptation, and innovation, a story that continues to.

Sardar Vallabh the nation's history, his legacy inextricably linked to the very idea of a unified and vision of a cohesive nation, bound by shared values and a common destiny. His unwavering resolve and political acumen were crucial in preventing the fragmentation of the newly independent nation. Patel understood that true strength lay not just in political independence, but also the larger framework of national unity. Patel's commitment to a unified India was not merely a political strategy; it was a deeply held conviction that a strong, united nation was essential for progress and prosperity. His actions, often firm and decisive, were guided by a vision of an India where regional differences were a source of strength,

Patel's most significant contribution to Indian unity was undoubtedly his role in integrating the princely states into the Indian Union. At the time of independence, India was not a homogenous entity, but rather a patchwork of British Indian provinces and over 560 autonomous princely states, each with its own ruler and varying degrees of independence. These states, theoretically free to accede to either India or Pakistan, or even remain independent, posed a grave threat to the nascent nation's territorial integrity. Patel, as the first Home Minister of India, was entrusted with the daunting task of persuading these princely states to join the Indian Union. He approached this challenge with a combination of diplomacy, persuasion, and, where necessary, a firm hand. He understood that a purely coercive approach would be counterproductive, potentially leading to widespread unrest and instability. Instead, he appealed to the patriotism of the rulers, emphasizing the shared history, culture, and destiny of their states with the rest of India. He assured them of fair treatment, guaranteeing them privy purses (annual payments) and certain privileges in exchange for ceding their sovereignty to the Indian Union. His persuasive skills were particularly evident in his negotiations with the rulers of states like Travancore, Bhopal, and Jodhpur, who initially harbored reservations about joining India. He patiently addressed their concerns, allaying their fears and convincing them of the benefits of integration. However, Patel was not averse to using a more assertive approach when necessary. In the case of Junagadh, a state with a Hindu majority but ruled by a Muslim Nawab who initially acceded to Pakistan, Patel orchestrated a plebiscite that overwhelmingly unity and his belief that the state's independence would pose a serious threat to India's security and stability. His firm stance sent a clear message to other princely states that India was determined to preserve its territorial integrity and would not tolerate any attempts at secession. The integration of the princely states was a monumental achievement that architect of Indian unity. His pragmatic approach, combining diplomacy with firmness, ensured the successful integration of diverse political entities into a single, cohesive nation.

Beyond the integration of princely states, Sardar Patel played a crucial role in maintaining law and order in the turbulent years following independence. The partition of India led to widespread communal violence and displacement, posing a significant challenge to the newly formed government. As Home Minister, Patel was responsible for maintaining peace and stability across the country. He took decisive steps to quell the violence, deploying security forces to affected areas and working with local leaders to restore calm. He also oversaw the rehabilitation of millions of refugees who had been displaced by the partition. Patel's firm hand in dealing with communal tensions earned him the respect of people from all communities. He was seen as a leader who was committed to protecting the lives and property of all citizens, regardless of their religion or caste. His commitment to secularism and his unwavering stance against communalism helped to prevent the further fragmentation of Indian society. Patel also played a key role in shaping the administrative structure of independent India. He recognized the need for a strong and efficient civil service to implement government policies and ensure effective governance. He worked to strengthen the Indian Administrative Service (IAS) and the Indian Police Service (IPS), ensuring that they were staffed by competent and dedicated officers. His efforts to build a strong and professional civil service laid the foundation for a stable and well-governed India. His actions demonstrated his commitment to building a strong and united India, capable of overcoming the challenges of independence.

The deeply with Sardar Patel's vision for the nation. This initiative, launched by the Government of India in 2015, aims to enhance interaction and promote mutual understanding between people of different states and union territories. It seeks to foster a sense encourages people to learn about the history, culture, and traditions of other states and union territories. This helps to break down stereotypes and promote a sense of shared identity. The initiative also emphasizes the importance of preserving and promoting India's diverse languages. It encourages people to learn languages other than their mother tongue, fostering communication and understanding between different is paramount.

Sardar Patel's vision extended beyond mere political integration; he understood that true unity required economic and social cohesion. He championed policies aimed at reducing regional disparities and promoting inclusive growth. He believed that a strong and prosperous India could only be built on the foundation of economic equality and social justice. Patel was a strong advocate for the development of infrastructure, particularly in rural areas. He recognized that improved infrastructure was essential for connecting remote regions to the mainstream economy and improving the lives of people living in those areas. He supported the construction of roads, railways, and irrigation projects, which helped to boost agricultural production and create employment opportunities. He also emphasized the importance of education and skill development, recognizing that these were crucial for empowering individuals and communities. Patel was a firm believer in the power of cooperatives to promote economic development and social upliftment. He encouraged the formation of cooperative societies in various sectors, such as agriculture, dairy, and textiles. He believed that cooperatives could empower farmers and artisans, providing them with access to credit, technology, and markets. He saw cooperatives as a tool for promoting self-reliance and reducing dependence on intermediaries. Patel's commitment to social justice was evident in his efforts to uplift the marginalized sections of society. He was a strong supporter of land reforms, aimed at redistributing land from wealthy landlords to landless peasants. He believed that land ownership was essential for economic empowerment and social dignity. He also worked to abolish untouchability and promote the welfare of Scheduled Castes and Scheduled Tribes. Patel's vision of economic and social cohesion remains relevant today. India still faces significant challenges in terms of regional disparities, poverty, and inequality. To achieve true unity and prosperity, it is essential to address these challenges and ensure that all citizens have access to opportunities for growth and development. His emphasis on infrastructure development, education, skill development, and social justice continues to guide policymakers and inspire social reformers. His vision serves as a reminder that true unity requires not only political integration but also economic and social cohesion, ensuring that all citizens have a stake in the nation's progress and prosperity.

Sardar Patel's leadership style was characterized by his pragmatism, decisiveness, and unwavering commitment to the national interest. He was a man of action, who believed in getting things done efficiently and effectively. He was not afraid to take tough decisions, even when they were unpopular. His ability to inspire confidence and trust in others was crucial to his success in integrating the princely states and maintaining law and order in the turbulent years following independence. Patel was a master strategist, who understood the importance of careful planning and execution. He was also a skilled negotiator, who could persuade people to see his point of view. His ability to build consensus and forge alliances was essential for achieving his goals. Patel was a strong believer in teamwork and collaboration. He surrounded himself with a team of competent and dedicated officials, who shared his vision for a united and prosperous India. He empowered his team members, giving them the freedom to take initiative and make decisions. His leadership style was characterized by his integrity, honesty, and selflessness. He was a man of impeccable character, who always put the national interest above his own personal gain. His commitment to public service and his dedication to the welfare of the people inspired generations of Indians. His leadership qualities continue to inspire leaders and policymakers today, reminding them of the importance of pragmatism, decisiveness, and unwavering commitment to the national interest.

Sardar Vallabhbhai Patel's life and work offer profound lessons for contemporary India commitment to national unity, his pragmatic approach to governance, and his inclusive vision for the nation remain deeply relevant in today's world. His legacy serves as a reminder that true strength lies in unity, and that differences should be celebrated as sources of strength rather than division. Patel's emphasis on economic and social cohesion is particularly important in a country as diverse as India. To achieve true unity and prosperity, it is essential to address regional disparities, promote inclusive growth, and ensure that all citizens have access to opportunities for advancement. His vision of a strong and united India, built on the foundations of economic equality and social justice, continues to inspire policymakers and social reformers. Patel's leadership style, characterized by pragmatism, decisiveness, and unwavering commitment to the national interest, provides a valuable model for leaders in all fields. His ability to inspire confidence and trust in others, his skill in building consensus, and his dedication to public service are qualities that are essential for effective leadership. his life serves as a reminder that true leadership requires integrity, honesty, and a willingness to put the needs of the nation above personal gain. Sardar Patel demonstrating the power of unity, diversity, and shared purpose in building a great nation.

India, a land celebrated for its kaleidoscopic tapestry of cultures, languages, religions, and traditions, stands embedded in the nation's ethos, transcends mere tolerance; it signifies a harmonious coexistence where differences are not just acknowledged but embraced as sources of strength and enrichment. In contemporary and opportunities. The pursuit of Vikasit Bharat necessitates a cohesive national identity, one that acknowledges and celebrates the multifaceted nature of its citizenry. Globalization, technological advancements, and socio-political shifts have brought both unprecedented opportunities and complex challenges to this delicate balance. Increased interconnectedness has fostered greater awareness and understanding of diverse cultures, yet it has also amplified the potential for cultural homogenization and the erosion of unique identities. Furthermore, socio-economic disparities, historical injustices, and the rise of identity politics pose significant threats to the fabric of unity. As India strives for economic prosperity and social progress, it is imperative to ensure that the benefits of development are equitably distributed and that marginalized communities are empowered to participate fully in the nation-building process. The concept of Unity in Diversity, therefore, becomes not just a philosophical ideal but a pragmatic necessity for achieving inclusive and sustainable development in the journey towards Vikasit Bharat. It requires a conscious and concerted effort to foster mutual respect, understanding, and empathy among all sections of society, while simultaneously addressing the root causes of division and inequality.

The historical and philosophical underpinnings of Unity in Diversity in India are deeply rooted in its ancient civilization, where diverse schools of thought, religious practices, and social customs have coexisted for centuries. From the Vedic period to the Mughal era and the British Raj, India has been a melting pot of cultures, with each wave of migration and conquest leaving its indelible markakti and Sufi movements further reinforced the ideals of inclusivity and social justice, transcending religious boundaries and promoting love, compassion, and equality. These movements challenged the rigid social hierarchies and orthodox religious practices, advocating for a more egalitarian and syncretic society. During the Indian independence movement, leaders like Mahatma Gandhi and Jawaharlal Nehru recognized the importance of Unity in Diversity as a cornerstone of nation-building. Gandhi's philosophy of Sarvodaya, or the welfare of all, emphasized the need to uplift the marginalized and ensure social and economic justice for all sections of society. Nehru, as the first Prime Minister of India, championed the idea of a secular and democratic nation, where all citizens, regardless of their religion, caste, or language, would have equal rights and opportunities. The Indian Constitution, adopted in 1950, enshrines these principles, guaranteeing fundamental rights and freedoms to all citizens and promoting social, economic, and political justice. The Constitution recognizes India as a secular state, ensuring freedom of religion and protecting the rights of minorities. It also promotes the development of all languages and cultures, recognizing the importance of linguistic and cultural diversity in strengthening national unity. The historical and philosophical context provides a strong foundation for understanding the significance of Unity in Diversity in contemporary India, highlighting the enduring values of tolerance, inclusivity, and social justice that have shaped the nation's identity and continue to guide its path towards progress and development.

Globalization and technological advancements have profoundly impacted the dynamics of Unity in Diversity in contemporary India, presenting both opportunities and challenges. Increased interconnectedness has facilitated greater cultural exchange and understanding, exposing people to diverse perspectives and ways of life. The rise of social media and digital platforms has enabled individuals and communities to connect across geographical boundaries, fostering dialogue and collaboration. However, globalization has also led to the homogenization of cultures, with the dominance of Western values and lifestyles posing a threat to local traditions and identities. The spread of consumerism and materialism has further eroded traditional values, leading to a sense of cultural alienation and loss of identity. Moreover, technological advancements have exacerbated existing inequalities, with the digital divide widening the gap between the rich and the poor, the urban and the rural. Access to technology and digital literacy remains a challenge for many marginalized communities, hindering their ability to participate fully in the digital economy and access information and opportunities. The rise of social media has also contributed to the spread of misinformation and hate speech, fueling social divisions and undermining trust in institutions. The anonymity afforded by online platforms has emboldened extremist groups and individuals to propagate divisive ideologies and incite violence against minority communities. Therefore, it is crucial to harness the power of technology for promoting inclusivity and social cohesion, while mitigating its negative impacts on cultural diversity and social harmony.

Socio-economic disparities and identity politics pose significant challenges to Unity in Diversity in contemporary India, hindering the nation's progress towards Vikasit Bharat. Despite significant economic growth in recent decades, inequalities persist, with a large proportion of the population still living in poverty and lacking access to basic amenities such as education, healthcare, and sanitation. These disparities often intersect with social identities, with marginalized communities such as Dalits, Adivasis, and religious minorities facing systemic discrimination and exclusion. The lack of economic opportunities and social mobility perpetuates cycles of poverty and inequality, fueling resentment and social unrest. Identity politics, based on caste, religion, language, and region, has become increasingly prominent in recent years, with political parties often exploiting social divisions for electoral gains. The rise of Hindu nationalism, in particular, has led to increased polarization and marginalization of religious minorities, undermining the secular fabric of the nation. The Citizenship Amendment Act (CAA) and the National Register of Citizens (NRC) have raised concerns about discrimination against Muslim citizens and the erosion of their rights. Furthermore, the increasing incidents of hate crimes and communal violence against minorities have created a climate of fear and insecurity, threatening social harmony and national unity. Addressing socio-economic disparities and identity politics requires a multi-pronged approach that includes promoting inclusive growth, ensuring social justice, and fostering a culture of tolerance and respect. Investing in education, healthcare, and skill development can empower marginalized communities and provide them with opportunities to improve their livelihoods. Implementing affirmative action policies and reservation systems can help to address historical injustices and ensure representation for underrepresented groups. Promoting interfaith dialogue and cultural exchange can foster understanding and empathy between different communities, while strengthening secular institutions and upholding the rule of law can protect the rights of all citizens. Overcoming these challenges is essential for building a more just, equitable, and harmonious society, where all citizens can thrive and contribute to the nation's progress. Therefore, concerted efforts are needed to promote social cohesion and bridge the divides that threaten to undermine the nation's unity.

The role of education and cultural exchange in promoting Unity in Diversity cannot be overstated, as they serve as powerful tools for fostering understanding, empathy, and mutual respect among different communities. Education plays a crucial role in shaping young minds and instilling values of tolerance, inclusivity, and social justice. Curricula should be designed to promote awareness of India's diverse cultures, histories, and traditions, while also addressing issues of discrimination and inequality. Encouraging critical thinking and dialogue can help students to challenge stereotypes and biases, fostering a more nuanced understanding of social realities. Cultural exchange programs, both within India and with other countries, can provide opportunities for people from different backgrounds to interact and learn from each other. These programs can include student exchanges, artist residencies, and cultural festivals, showcasing the richness and diversity of human expression. Promoting multilingualism and encouraging the study of different languages can also help to break down communication barriers and foster greater understanding between communities. Recognizing and celebrating the contributions of different cultures to India's heritage can strengthen national identity and promote a sense of belonging for all citizens. Investing in education and cultural exchange is essential for building a more inclusive and harmonious society, where diversity is celebrated as a source of strength and enrichment. These initiatives are vital for nurturing a generation that values diversity and works towards building a more united and prosperous nation.

Government policies and initiatives play a crucial role in fostering and safeguarding Unity in Diversity, requiring a multi-faceted approach that addresses social, economic, and political dimensions. The government must ensure that all citizens have equal access to opportunities and resources, regardless of their caste, religion, gender, or region. This includes implementing policies that promote inclusive growth, reduce inequality, and provide social safety nets for vulnerable populations. Affirmative action policies, such as reservations in education and employment, can help to address historical injustices and ensure representation for marginalized communities. However, these policies must be carefully designed and implemented to avoid unintended consequences and ensure that they benefit those who need them most. Protecting the rights of minorities and ensuring their safety and security is paramount. This requires strengthening law enforcement agencies, promoting interfaith dialogue, and taking strict action against hate speech and communal violence. The government should also promote cultural diversity through various initiatives, such as supporting cultural festivals, preserving historical sites, and promoting the study of different languages and cultures. Recognizing and celebrating the contributions of different communities to India's heritage can strengthen national identity and promote a sense of belonging for all citizens. Promoting decentralization and empowering local communities can also help to foster Unity in Diversity. By giving local communities more control over their resources and decision-making processes, the government can ensure that their voices are heard and that their needs are met. This can also help to reduce regional disparities and promote a sense of ownership and responsibility among citizens. The government should also promote transparency and accountability in governance, ensuring that all citizens have access to information and that their grievances are addressed promptly and effectively. By promoting good governance and upholding the rule of law, the government can build trust and confidence among citizens, fostering a more cohesive and harmonious society. These measures are essential for building a strong and united nation, where all citizens can thrive and contribute to the nation's progress towards Vikasit Bharat. Therefore, the government's commitment to these principles is vital for realizing the vision of a prosperous and inclusive India.

As India strives towards becoming a Vikasit Bharat, the principle of Unity in

Diversity remains a cornerstone of its progress and prosperity. It is not merely a slogan but a lived reality that has shaped the nation's identity and continues to guide its path forward. Embracing diversity requires a conscious and continuous effort from all stakeholders, including the government, civil society, and individual citizens. Addressing socio-economic disparities, promoting inclusive growth, and ensuring social justice are essential for creating a level playing field for all. Investing in education, promoting cultural exchange, and fostering interfaith dialogue can help to break down barriers and build bridges between communities. Government policies and initiatives must be designed to protect the rights of minorities, promote cultural diversity, and empower local communities. The challenges posed by globalization, technological advancements, and identity politics must be addressed proactively, with a focus on promoting inclusivity, social cohesion, and responsible citizenship. The vision of Vikasit Bharat can only be realized if all citizens feel a sense of belonging and have the opportunity to participate fully in the nation-building process. By embracing Unity in Diversity, India can unlock its full potential and emerge as a global leader, setting an example for other nations to follow. The journey towards a developed and inclusive India requires a collective commitment to the values of tolerance, empathy, and mutual respect, ensuring that no one is left behind in the pursuit of progress and prosperity.

India, a land of unparalleled diversity, stands as a testament to the harmonious coexistence of myriad India, Great India) initiative, launched by the Government of India, seeks to further strengthen this bond by fostering mutual understanding and appreciation among the diverse states and union territories of the country. This initiative recognizes that true national integration transcends mere political unity and necessitates a deeper cultural and emotional connect among its citizens. It aims to achieve this by promoting reciprocal interactions between different states, encouraging the exchange of ideas,

The concept has shaped India's socio-cultural and political landscape for centuries. It acknowledges the existence of a multitude of distinct cultural identities, languages, religions, customs, and traditions within the geographical boundaries of India, while simultaneously emphasizing the underlying unity that binds them together as a nation. This unity is not about homogenization or the suppression of differences but rather about celebrating and respecting the unique contributions of each constituent group to the collective identity of India. The historical roots of this concept can be traced back to ancient India, where various kingdoms and empires coexisted, each with its own distinct cultural and administrative systems. Despite their differences, these entities were interconnected through trade, religious exchanges, and shared philosophical traditions. The Mauryan Empire, for instance, encompassed a vast territory with diverse populations, yet it maintained a unified administrative structure and promoted a common ethical framework based on Buddhist principles. Similarly, the Mughal Empire, while being secularism, and federalism. The Constitution guarantees equal rights and opportunities to all citizens, regardless of their religion, race, caste, sex, or place of birth. It also recognizes the right of religious minorities to establish and administer their own educational institutions. The principle of federalism ensures that power is distributed between the central government andism, regionalism, and linguistic chauvinism continue to pose threats to national integration. The rise of religious fundamentalism and extremist ideologies has also led to increased social polarization and violence. Addressing these challenges requires a multi-pronged approach that includes promoting education, fostering interfaith dialogue, strengthening democratic institutions, and ensuring inclusive economic growth. It also necessitates a conscious effort to combat prejudice and discrimination and to promote a culture of tolerance and respect for diversity. The enduring strength of India lies in its ability to embrace its differences and forge a common identity based on shared values and aspirations.

The initiative aims to promote a deeper understanding and appreciation of the diverse cultures, traditions, languages, and histories of different states and union territories. This is achieved through a variety of activities, including cultural exchange programs, student exchange programs, tourism promotion, and the sharing of best practices in various fields. For example, pairing one state with another to promote cultural understanding through festivals, exhibitions, and performances. Students from different states are encouraged to visit and study in other parts of the country, fostering a sense of national unity and integration. The initiative also promotes tourism to different states, showcasing their unique attractions and cultural heritage. States are encouraged to share their best practices in areas such as education, healthcare, and economic development, promoting mutual learning and growth. The initiative also leverages digital platforms and social media to disseminate information about the diverse cultures and traditions of different states, reaching a wider audience and promoting greater awareness. By fostering greater understanding and appreciation of India's diversity, the initiative aims to strengthen the bonds of unity and promote a sense of shared identity among its citizens.

India tapestry of cultures, languages, religions, and traditions. This inherent diversity, far, but a lived reality that permeates every facet of Indian society, shaping its social fabric and contributing significantly to its unique character. This introduction explores the profound social dimension of India's unity in diversity, examining how it fosters social cohesion, promotes inclusivity, and fuels innovation. It delves into the historical context that has shaped this unique characteristic, acknowledging the challenges and triumphs encountered along the way. Furthermore, it investigates how this social strength contributes to India's global standing, enhancing its soft power and fostering cross-cultural understanding. By understanding the intricate interplay between unity and diversity in the Indian context, we gain valuable insights into the resilience and adaptability of its society. This exploration will highlight how embracing differences, fostering dialogue, and promoting mutual respect are essential ingredients for building a strong, vibrant, and truly incredible Bharat. The following sections will delve deeper into specific examples and analyze the impact of this social dimension on various aspects of Indian life.

India's historical trajectory has profoundly shaped its unique social fabric, characterized by a remarkable unity in diversity. The subcontinent has been a melting pot of civilizations, witnessing the confluence of various cultures, religions, and ethnicities over millennia. From the ancient Indus Valley Civilization to the arrival of Indo-Aryans, the Mauryan Empire, the Mughal era, and the British colonial period, each epoch has left an indelible mark on the social landscape of India. The interactions and exchanges between these diverse groups have resulted in a rich tapestry of customs, traditions, languages, and beliefs. The spirit of accommodation and assimilation has been a defining feature of Indian society, allowing different communities to coexist and contribute to the collective identity. This historical process has fostered a sense of shared heritage and a deep appreciation for the country's pluralistic ethos. Religious diversity is particularly prominent in India, with Hinduism, Islam, Sikhism, Christianity, Buddhism, Jainism, and Zoroastrianism coexisting for centuries. The interactions between these religions have led to the emergence of syncretic traditions and philosophies, such as Sufism and the Bhakti movement, which emphasize love, devotion, and the unity of all beings. These movements have played a crucial role in bridging social divides and promoting interfaith harmony. The caste system, a hierarchical social structure that has historically divided Indian society, presents a significant challenge to the ideal of unity in diversity. While the caste system has been outlawed and efforts have been made to address its discriminatory effects, its legacy continues to impact social relations and economic opportunities. Overcoming the deeply entrenched inequalities associated with caste remains a critical task for building a truly inclusive and equitable society. Despite the challenges posed by caste and other forms of social stratification, India's historical experience has instilled a remarkable capacity for adaptation, resilience, and social cohesion. The ability to navigate differences, negotiate competing interests, and forge a collective identity has been essential for maintaining social harmony and promoting national unity. This historical legacy continues to shape India's social dimension, influencing its approach to governance, development, and international relations. The echoes of the past resonate in the present, reminding us of the importance of preserving and celebrating the country's rich cultural heritage while striving for a more just and.

The social cohesion fostered by unity in diversity plays a crucial role in India's economic progress and innovation. When people from different backgrounds, experiences, and perspectives come together, they bring a wealth of knowledge and skills to the table. This diversity of thought can spark creativity, challenge conventional wisdom, and lead to the development of novel solutions to complex problems. In the workplace, diverse teams are often more productive and innovative than homogenous teams. They are better able to understand and cater to the needs of a diverse customer base, adapt to changing market conditions, and generate new ideas. India's thriving IT sector, for example, is a testament to the power of diversity-driven innovation. Professionals from various regions, religions, and social backgrounds collaborate to create cutting-edge technologies and provide services to clients around the world. Beyond the IT sector, diversity also fuels innovation in other industries, such as manufacturing, healthcare, and education. When entrepreneurs, researchers, and policymakers embrace diversity and create inclusive environments, they unlock the full potential of India's human capital. Furthermore, social cohesion promotes economic stability and reduces the risk of conflict. When people feel a sense of belonging and shared identity, they are more likely to cooperate, invest in their communities, and participate in the democratic process. This, in turn, creates a more stable and predictable environment for businesses to operate and grow. In contrast, societies that are divided along ethnic, religious, or linguistic lines are more prone to conflict, which can disrupt economic activity and undermine development efforts. By fostering unity in diversity, India can create a more inclusive and prosperous society for all its citizens. This approach not only benefits the economy but also strengthens social bonds and promotes a sense of national pride. The synergy between diverse talents and perspectives propels India forward on its path of economic development and global competitiveness.

India's unity in diversity significantly enhances its soft power and global standing. The country's rich cultural heritage, encompassing diverse art forms, music, dance, literature, and philosophy, attracts people from all over the world. This cultural richness serves as a powerful tool for promoting cross-cultural understanding and fostering positive relationships with other nations. Indian cinema, particularly Bollywood, has a massive global following, transcending linguistic and cultural barriers. Indian films showcase the country's diverse traditions, values, and social realities, providing audiences with a glimpse into the heart and soul of India. Similarly, Indian cuisine, with its myriad flavors and regional variations, has gained immense popularity worldwide, becoming a symbol of India's culinary diversity. Yoga and Ayurveda, ancient Indian practices that promote physical and mental well-being, have also gained widespread acceptance and are recognized for their holistic benefits. These cultural exports contribute to India's soft power by creating a positive image of the country and fostering goodwill among people of different nationalities. Furthermore, India's commitment to democracy, pluralism, and the rule of law enhances its credibility and influence on the global stage. As the world's largest democracy, India serves as a model for other developing countries aspiring to build inclusive and democratic societies. India's active participation in international forums, such as the United Nations, the G20, and the BRICS, demonstrates its commitment to multilateralism and its willingness to work with other nations to address global challenges. India's growing economic strength and its contributions to global innovation further enhance its standing in the world. The country's emergence as a major economic power has given it a greater voice in international affairs and has allowed it to play a more prominent role in shaping the global agenda. India's unique blend of cultural richness, democratic values, and economic dynamism positions it as a key player in the 21st century, capable of contributing to a more peaceful, prosperous, and interconnected world. This multifaceted approach strengthens India's position as a responsible and influential global citizen.

Despite the numerous benefits of unity in diversity, India faces significant challenges in fully realizing its potential. Social inequalities based on caste, religion, gender, and socioeconomic status continue to persist, hindering the country's progress towards becoming a truly inclusive society. Discrimination and prejudice against marginalized communities remain a reality, limiting their access to education, employment, and other opportunities. Addressing these inequalities requires a multi-pronged approach that includes strengthening legal frameworks, promoting affirmative action policies, and fostering greater social awareness. Religious polarization and communal tensions pose a serious threat to social harmony and national unity. The rise of religious extremism and intolerance can lead to violence, discrimination, and the erosion of secular values. Promoting interfaith dialogue, fostering mutual respect, and combating hate speech are essential for maintaining peace and harmony in a diverse society. Economic disparities also contribute to social divisions. The gap between the rich and the poor continues to widen, creating resentment and social unrest. Ensuring equitable access to education, healthcare, and economic opportunities is crucial for reducing inequality and promoting social justice. Furthermore, promoting inclusive governance and empowering local communities are essential for addressing the challenges of diversity. Decentralization of power, participatory decision-making, and the protection of minority rights can help to build trust and foster a sense of belonging among all citizens. Overcoming these challenges requires a collective effort from the government, civil society, and individuals. By working together to promote equality, justice, and social harmony, India can unlock its full potential and build a truly incredible Bharat. This collaborative spirit is essential for navigating the complexities of a diverse society and ensuring a brighter future for all.

To further strengthen the social dimension of unity in diversity, India needs to prioritize education, promote intercultural dialogue, and foster inclusive policies. Education plays a vital role in shaping attitudes, promoting understanding, and fostering empathy. By incorporating diverse perspectives and histories into the curriculum, schools can help students develop a deeper appreciation for India's rich cultural heritage and the importance of inclusivity. Promoting critical thinking skills and encouraging open discussions about social issues can also help students challenge stereotypes and biases. Intercultural dialogue is essential for building bridges between different communities and fostering mutual respect. Creating platforms for people from diverse backgrounds to interact, share their experiences, and learn from each other can help to break down barriers and promote understanding. This can be achieved through community events, cultural festivals, and online forums. Inclusive policies are crucial for ensuring that all citizens have equal access to opportunities and are treated with dignity and respect. This includes implementing affirmative action policies to address historical injustices, enacting anti-discrimination laws to protect marginalized communities, and promoting gender equality. It also requires creating a more inclusive political system that ensures representation for all segments of society. Furthermore, promoting multilingualism and protecting linguistic diversity are essential for preserving India's cultural heritage. Supporting the development and promotion of regional languages can help to foster a sense of identity and belonging among different communities. Encouraging the use of multiple languages in education and public life can also promote intercultural understanding and communication. Finally, promoting media literacy and combating misinformation are crucial for safeguarding social harmony. The spread of fake news and hate speech can incite violence and undermine trust in institutions. By empowering citizens to critically evaluate information and promoting responsible journalism, India can create a more informed and resilient society. These proactive measures are vital for nurturing a society where diversity is not just tolerated but celebrated as a source of strength and innovation.

India's unity in diversity is not merely a slogan but a lived reality that shapes its social fabric, fuels its economic progress, enhances its global standing, and defines its unique identity. This inherent diversity, born from a rich historical tapestry and nurtured by a spirit of accommodation, has fostered social cohesion, promoted innovation, and strengthened the nation's resilience. However, the journey towards a truly inclusive and equitable society is ongoing. Challenges such as social inequalities, religious polarization, and economic disparities persist, requiring sustained efforts to address them. By prioritizing education, promoting intercultural dialogue, fostering inclusive policies, and empowering marginalized communities, India can overcome these challenges and unlock its full potential. The path forward requires a collective commitment from the government, civil society, and individuals to uphold the values of equality, justice, and social harmony. Embracing diversity as a source of strength, fostering mutual respect, and promoting understanding are essential ingredients for building a strong, vibrant, and truly incredible Bharat. As India continues to evolve and navigate the complexities of the 21st century, its ability to harness the power of unity in diversity will be crucial for achieving its aspirations and contributing to a more peaceful, prosperous, and interconnected world. The future of India lies in its ability to celebrate its differences, bridge its divides, and forge a common destiny based on the principles of inclusivity and shared prosperity.

India, often diversity, encompassing a multitude of languages, religions, cultures, and ethnicities, is not merely a demographic reality but a foundational characteristic that shapes the nation's political landscape. The political uphold of this unity is a complex and ongoing process, demanding constant negotiation, adaptation, and a commitment to inclusive governance. The Indian political system, with its democratic framework, strives to accommodate this vast spectrum of differences, ensuring representation and participation for all its citizens. This introduction will explore the intricate ways in which India's political structures and processes navigate the challenges and opportunities presented by its diverse population, examining the mechanisms that uphold unity while respecting and celebrating its inherent heterogeneity.

The Indian Constitution serves as the cornerstone of political unity amidst diversity, providing a framework of fundamental rights and directive principles that aim to ensure equality and justice for all citizens. Enshrined within its articles are provisions that protect religious freedom, cultural expression, and linguistic rights, acknowledging and safeguarding the diverse identities that constitute the Indian nation. The Constitution's commitment to secularism, for instance, seeks to maintain a neutral stance towards all religions, preventing the dominance of any single faith and fostering an environment of mutual respect and tolerance. Furthermore, affirmative action policies, such as reservations for Scheduled Castes, Scheduled Tribes, and Other Backward Classes, attempt to address historical inequalities and promote social inclusion, ensuring that marginalized communities have access to education, employment, and political representation. The electoral system, based on universal adult suffrage, empowers every citizen to participate in the democratic process, regardless of their caste, creed, religion, or gender. This inclusive approach to political participation allows diverse voices to be heard and represented in the government, fostering a sense of ownership and belonging among the populace. Political parties, often formed along regional or ideological lines, play a crucial role in articulating the interests and aspirations of different communities, contributing to a vibrant and competitive political landscape. The judiciary, as an independent and impartial arbiter, safeguards the Constitution and ensures that the rights of all citizens are protected, providing a mechanism for resolving disputes and upholding the rule of law. These constitutional and institutional mechanisms are vital in maintaining the delicate balance between unity and diversity in the Indian polity.

However, the path to upholding political unity in a diverse nation like India is not without its challenges. Regionalism, communalism, and caste-based politics often pose significant threats to social cohesion and national integration. The assertion of regional identities and demands for greater autonomy can sometimes lead to conflicts with the central government, testing the resilience of the federal structure. The exploitation of religious sentiments for political gain can exacerbate social divisions and undermine the secular fabric of the nation. Caste-based discrimination, despite being outlawed, continues to persist in various forms, hindering social mobility and perpetuating inequalities. Moreover, economic disparities and uneven development across different regions can fuel discontent and resentment, further complicating the task of maintaining unity. The rise of identity politics, while empowering marginalized communities, can also lead to fragmentation and polarization if not managed carefully. Effective governance, inclusive policies, and a commitment to social justice are essential to address these challenges and prevent them from undermining the foundations of national unity. The media and civil society organizations also play a crucial role in promoting dialogue, fostering understanding, and holding the government accountable. Addressing these persistent challenges requires a multi-pronged approach that strengthens democratic institutions, promotes inclusive growth, and fosters a sense of shared citizenship.

Looking ahead, the political uphold of unity in diversity in India requires a renewed focus on strengthening democratic institutions, promoting inclusive development, and fostering a culture of tolerance and mutual respect. Investing in education and skill development is crucial to empower citizens from all backgrounds and provide them with equal opportunities to participate in the economy and society. Promoting inter-community dialogue and cultural exchange programs can help to bridge divides and foster a sense of shared identity. Strengthening local governance and empowering communities to manage their own affairs can promote greater participation and accountability. Addressing economic disparities and ensuring equitable access to resources and opportunities is essential to reduce social tensions and promote inclusive growth. Furthermore, promoting responsible media and combating misinformation are crucial to prevent the spread of hate speech and divisive narratives. The role of technology and social media in shaping public discourse needs to be carefully managed to ensure that it promotes constructive engagement and does not exacerbate social divisions.

The initiative plays a crucial role in promoting national integration and strengthening the social fabric of India. By fostering greater understanding and appreciation of diversity, it helps to break down stereotypes and prejudices, promoting a culture of tolerance and respect. This is particularly important in a country like India, where social divisions based on caste, religion, language, and region can often lead to conflict and discrimination. The initiative provides a platform for people from different backgrounds to interact with each other, share their experiences, and learn from one another. This helps to build bridges between communities and promote a sense of shared identity. It also encourages people to celebrate their differences and to recognize the value of diversity as a source of strength. Moreover, the initiative promotes a sense of national pride and belonging, encouraging citizens to actively participate in the development of the country. By fostering a sense of unity and common purpose, it helps to create a more cohesive and resilient society. The initiative also contributes to the economic development of the country by promoting tourism, trade, and investment. By showcasing the diverse attractions and cultural heritage of different states, it attracts tourists from all over the world, generating revenue and creating employment opportunities. It also facilitates the exchange of goods and services between different states, promoting economic growth and integration. Furthermore, the initiative encourages investment in different parts of the country, creating new opportunities for businesses and entrepreneurs. The initiative also promotes social harmony and reduces the risk of conflict and violence. By fostering greater understanding and appreciation of diversity, it helps to prevent the spread of hate speech and misinformation, which can often lead to social unrest. It also encourages people to resolve their differences peacefully and to work together to build a more just and equitable society. The initiative serves as a powerful tool for promoting national unity, social cohesion, and economic development.

While the initiative has made significant strides in promoting unity and understanding, it also faces several challenges. One of the main challenges is the persistence of stereotypes and prejudices, which can hinder effective communication and collaboration between different groups. Overcoming these biases requires sustained efforts to promote education, awareness, and cross-cultural dialogue. Another challenge is the uneven distribution of resources and opportunities across different states and regions. This can lead to feelings of resentment and marginalization, undermining the sense of national unity. Addressing these disparities requires targeted interventions to promote inclusive growth and development in all parts of the country. Furthermore, the initiative needs to be more effectively integrated into the education system, so that young people are exposed to the diverse cultures and traditions of India from an early age. This will help to foster a sense of national identity and belonging among future generations. The initiative also needs to be more inclusive of marginalized communities, such as tribal groups and religious minorities, ensuring that their voices are heard and their concerns are addressed. By addressing these challenges, the initiative can further strengthen its impact and contribute to building a more united, prosperous, and equitable India.

To maximize the impact of the initiative, several recommendations can be considered. Firstly, there is a need to strengthen the institutional framework for implementing and monitoring the initiative. This includes establishing clear goals and objectives, developing measurable indicators of progress, and ensuring adequate funding and resources. It also requires greater coordination and collaboration between different government departments and agencies, as well as with civil society organizations and the private sector. Secondly, the initiative should be expanded to include a wider range of activities and programs, such as language exchange programs, joint research projects, and cultural festivals. These activities should be designed to promote greater interaction and understanding between people from different backgrounds, fostering a sense of shared identity and belonging. Thirdly, the initiative should leverage technology and digital platforms to reach a wider audience and promote greater awareness of India's diversity. This includes creating online resources, developing mobile apps, and using social media to disseminate information and engage with citizens. Fourthly, the initiative should focus on promoting inclusive growth and development, ensuring that all communities benefit from the economic progress of the country. This requires targeted interventions to address disparities in education, healthcare, and employment opportunities, particularly for marginalized groups. Fifthly, the initiative should promote greater citizen participation and engagement, encouraging people to take ownership of the program and contribute to its success. This includes creating opportunities for people to volunteer, participate in decision-making processes, and share their experiences and ideas. By implementing these recommendations, the initiative can be further strengthened and its impact on promoting national unity, social cohesion, and economic development can be maximized.

The initiative represents a significant step towards realizing the vision of a united and prosperous India, where diversity is celebrated and all citizens have the opportunity to thrive. It underscores the importance of fostering mutual understanding, respect, and appreciation among the diverse communities that make up the nation. By promoting cultural exchange, educational initiatives, and economic cooperation, the initiative strengthens the bonds of unity and promotes a sense of shared identity. However, the success of the initiative depends on sustained efforts to address the challenges that remain, such as the persistence of stereotypes and prejudices, the uneven distribution of resources and opportunities, and the need for greater inclusivity and citizen participation. Overcoming these obstacles requires a multi-pronged approach that involves government, civil society, and the private sector working together to promote education, awareness, and inclusive growth. The initiative serves as a reminder that true national integration is not about homogenization or the suppression of differences, but rather about embracing diversity as a source of strength and celebrating the unique contributions of each community to the collective identity of India. It is a call to action for all citizens to actively participate in building a more united, prosperous, and equitable nation, where everyone has the opportunity to reach their full potential. The continued commitment to the principles of the initiative will undoubtedly pave the way for a brighter future for India, one where unity in diversity is not just a slogan, but a lived reality.

India, a land of unparalleled diversity, stands as a testament to the harmonious coexistence of myriad cultures, languages

India's cultural diversity, a vibrant mosaic woven from a multitude of languages, religions, traditions, and artistic expressions, serves as a potent engine for innovation and creativity. This rich heterogeneity fosters a dynamic environment where diverse perspectives converge, sparking novel ideas and approaches across various sectors. The cross-pollination of thoughts and practices from different cultural backgrounds fuels ingenuity, leading to the development of unique solutions tailored to the specific needs and challenges of the nation. The linguistic diversity of India, with its myriad dialects and languages, acts as a catalyst for creativity in literature, music, and performing arts. Each language carries with it a unique cultural heritage, preserving ancient stories, philosophical insights, and artistic traditions. This linguistic richness not only enriches the nation's cultural landscape but also provides a fertile ground for innovation in creative industries. The fusion of different musical styles, literary themes, and artistic techniques from various linguistic regions gives rise to new and innovative forms of expression, captivating audiences both within India and across the globe. Furthermore, India's religious diversity, encompassing Hinduism, Islam, Christianity, Sikhism, Buddhism, Jainism, and Zoroastrianism, promotes a culture of tolerance, understanding, and mutual respect. This interfaith harmony fosters a peaceful environment where individuals from different religious backgrounds can coexist and collaborate, contributing to the nation's social and economic progress.

The shared values of compassion, empathy, and service, common to all religions, inspire individuals to work together for the betterment of society, addressing social issues such as poverty, inequality, and discrimination. The celebration of religious festivals and traditions from different faiths provides opportunities for cultural exchange and understanding, strengthening the bonds of unity and harmony among diverse communities. Moreover, the diversity of culinary traditions across India, with each region boasting its unique flavors, ingredients, and cooking techniques, fuels innovation in the food industry. The fusion of different culinary styles and ingredients from various regions gives rise to new and exciting culinary creations, catering to the evolving tastes and preferences of consumers. The growing popularity of regional cuisines in urban areas and the increasing demand for authentic Indian food in international markets demonstrate the innovative potential of India's culinary diversity. The food processing industry, leveraging the diverse agricultural produce of the country, develops innovative food products that cater to both domestic and international markets, contributing to the nation's economic growth.

India's diverse ecosystem, encompassing a wide range of geographical features, climatic conditions, and natural resources, fosters resilience and adaptability in the face of environmental challenges. The country's varied agricultural practices, adapted to different agro-climatic zones, ensure food security and livelihood opportunities for millions of farmers. The traditional knowledge systems, developed over centuries by indigenous communities, provide sustainable solutions for resource management and climate change adaptation. The conservation efforts, driven by local communities and supported by government initiatives, protect biodiversity and preserve the ecological balance. The development of drought-resistant crops, water-efficient irrigation techniques, and renewable energy sources, tailored to the specific needs of different regions, enhances the resilience of communities to climate-related risks. The promotion of eco-tourism, showcasing the natural beauty and cultural heritage of diverse regions, generates income opportunities for local communities while promoting environmental conservation. The integration of traditional knowledge with modern technologies, such as remote sensing and geographic information systems, improves the monitoring and management of natural resources. The establishment of protected areas, such as national parks and wildlife sanctuaries, safeguards biodiversity and provides ecosystem services. The implementation of policies promoting sustainable agriculture, renewable energy, and waste management reduces the environmental footprint and promotes a green economy. The collaborative efforts of government agencies, research institutions, and civil society organizations strengthen the nation's capacity to address environmental challenges and build a sustainable future. This multifaceted approach to environmental stewardship ensures the long-term well-being of both the environment and the communities that depend on it.

India's commitment to inclusive growth, ensuring that the benefits of economic development reach all sections of society, is strengthened by its diverse social fabric. The government's affirmative action policies, such as reservations in education and employment for marginalized communities, promote social justice and equality of opportunity. The focus on skill development and entrepreneurship, particularly among women and youth from disadvantaged backgrounds, empowers individuals to participate in the economic growth story. The promotion of financial inclusion, through initiatives such as Jan Dhan Yojana, provides access to banking services for the unbanked population, enabling them to save, invest, and access credit. The strengthening of social safety nets, such as the National Rural Employment Guarantee Act (NREGA), provides livelihood security for vulnerable households. The investment in education and healthcare, particularly in rural and underserved areas, improves human capital and reduces inequalities. The promotion of digital literacy, through initiatives such as Digital India, bridges the digital divide and empowers citizens to access information and services online. The empowerment of local self-governments, through decentralization and devolution of powers, ensures that development priorities are aligned with the needs and aspirations of local communities. The promotion of social harmony and inter-community dialogue, through initiatives such as Ek Bharat Shreshtha Bharat, strengthens the bonds of unity and promotes mutual understanding. The collaborative efforts of government agencies, civil society organizations, and the private sector create a more equitable and inclusive society, where all citizens have the opportunity to thrive. This dedication to inclusivity ensures that no one is left behind in the nation's journey towards progress and prosperity.

India's diverse diaspora, spread across the globe, serves as a valuable asset in promoting the nation's interests and fostering international cooperation. The Indian diaspora acts as a bridge between India and the rest of the world, promoting cultural exchange, economic partnerships, and technological collaborations. The remittances sent by the diaspora contribute significantly to the Indian economy, supporting families and communities back home. The diaspora's expertise and knowledge in various fields contribute to India's development, through knowledge transfer, investment, and philanthropy. The diaspora's advocacy for India's interests in international forums strengthens the nation's global standing and influence. The government's engagement with the diaspora, through initiatives such as Pravasi Bharatiya Divas, strengthens the bonds of connection and fosters a sense of belonging. The promotion of Indian culture and values by the diaspora in their adopted countries enhances India's soft power and cultural diplomacy. The diaspora's role in promoting tourism to India contributes to the growth of the tourism sector and generates employment opportunities. The diaspora's investment in Indian businesses and startups fuels innovation and economic growth. The diaspora's philanthropic contributions support various social causes in India, such as education, healthcare, and poverty alleviation. The collaborative efforts of the government, the diaspora, and other stakeholders strengthen India's engagement with the world and promote its interests on the global stage. This global network of individuals with Indian roots contributes significantly to the nation's progress and prosperity, both at home and abroad.

Effective governance and policy frameworks are crucial for harnessing the potential of India's diversity and channeling it towards national development. The government's commitment to cooperative federalism, fostering collaboration between the center and the states, ensures that policies are tailored to the specific needs and priorities of different regions. The emphasis on evidence-based policymaking, utilizing data and research to inform decisions, improves the effectiveness and efficiency of government interventions. The promotion of transparency and accountability in governance, through initiatives such as the Right to Information Act, enhances public trust and reduces corruption. The strengthening of institutions, such as the judiciary and the election commission, ensures the rule of law and protects democratic values. The investment in infrastructure, such as roads, railways, and airports, improves connectivity and facilitates economic integration. The promotion of innovation and technology, through initiatives such as Startup India and Digital India, fosters a culture of entrepreneurship and drives economic growth. The simplification of regulations and procedures, reducing bureaucratic hurdles, improves the ease of doing business and attracts investment. The promotion of sustainable development, through policies that protect the environment and promote social equity, ensures that economic growth is inclusive and environmentally responsible. The collaborative efforts of government agencies, civil society organizations, and the private sector create a conducive environment for development and progress. This strategic approach to governance ensures that India's diversity is leveraged effectively to achieve its developmental goals and aspirations.

India's journey towards becoming a developed nation is inextricably linked to its ability to leverage its inherent unity in diversity. The nation's cultural richness, ecological diversity, and inclusive ethos provide a strong foundation for innovation, resilience, and sustainable growth. By embracing its diverse strengths and addressing its challenges with strategic policies and collaborative efforts, India can unlock its full potential and achieve its developmental goals. The continued focus on promoting social harmony, economic equity, and environmental sustainability will be crucial in ensuring that the benefits of progress reach all sections of society. The empowerment of local communities, the promotion of innovation and entrepreneurship, and the strengthening of governance institutions will be essential in driving inclusive and sustainable development. The engagement with the global community, through cultural exchange, economic partnerships, and technological collaborations, will further enhance India's progress and prosperity. The commitment to preserving its cultural heritage, protecting its natural resources, and promoting its values of peace, tolerance, and compassion will solidify India's position as a responsible and influential global leader. As India moves forward on its path of development, it must remain mindful of its unique identity and its responsibility to contribute to a more just and sustainable world. The nation's success in harnessing its diversity will not only transform its own future but also inspire other nations to embrace the power of unity in diversity for the betterment of humanity. India's story serves as a powerful reminder that diversity is not a weakness but a source of strength, innovation, and resilience, capable of shaping a brighter future for all.

India, a land of staggering contrasts and vibrant pluralities, stands at the cusp of transformative development, aspiring to become a 'Vikasit Bharat' – a developed India. This ambition, however, is inextricably linked to its unique socio-cultural fabric, characterized by unparalleled unity in diversity. The very essence of India lies in its ability to harmoniously integrate a multitude of ethnicities, religions, languages, and traditions, fostering a collective identity that transcends individual differences. This inherent unity, born from centuries of shared history and cultural exchange, presents both a profound opportunity and a significant challenge in the nation's developmental journey. The path to 'Vikasit Bharat' cannot be a monolithic, top-down imposition of a singular development model. Instead, it must be a nuanced and inclusive process that leverages the strengths of its diverse communities, recognizing their unique needs and aspirations. This requires a paradigm shift from viewing diversity as a hurdle to recognizing it as a valuable asset, a wellspring of innovation, resilience, and adaptability. By embracing its multifaceted identity, India can unlock its full potential, fostering a development trajectory that is not only economically robust but Also socially just and culturally enriching. The journey towards 'Vikasit Bharat' is thus a journey of collective empowerment, where every citizen, irrespective of their background, contributes to and benefits from the nation's progress, bound together by the enduring spirit of unity in diversity.

Harnessing the power of India's diverse human capital is paramount to achieving 'Vikasit Bharat'. Each region, community, and social group possesses unique skills, knowledge systems, and entrepreneurial spirit that can be strategically leveraged for economic growth. For instance, traditional artisans and craftspeople, repositories of centuries-old techniques and designs, can be empowered through skill development programs, access to markets, and technological interventions to enhance their productivity and competitiveness. Similarly, the agricultural sector, characterized by diverse farming practices and crop varieties across different agro-climatic zones, can benefit from tailored interventions that promote sustainable agriculture, improve yields, and enhance the livelihoods of farmers. Furthermore, India's linguistic diversity presents a unique opportunity to foster innovation in areas such as translation technology, content creation, and language-based services, creating new avenues for employment and economic growth. Recognizing and valuing the contributions of marginalized communities, including women, Scheduled Castes, Scheduled Tribes, and religious minorities, is crucial for ensuring inclusive development. These groups often face systemic barriers to education, healthcare, and economic opportunities, hindering their ability to participate fully in the nation's progress. Targeted interventions, such as affirmative action policies, skill development programs, and access to credit and financial services, can help to address these inequalities and empower marginalized communities to realize their full potential. Moreover, promoting social harmony and inter-community dialogue is essential for fostering a sense of belonging and shared citizenship, creating an environment conducive to inclusive growth and development. By investing in its diverse human capital and ensuring that all citizens have equal opportunities to thrive, India can unlock its full potential and accelerate its journey towards 'Vikasit Bharat'. This strategic approach ensures that the benefits of progress are shared equitably across all segments of society, fostering a more just and prosperous nation.

India's cultural diversity, a vibrant tapestry woven from myriad traditions, art forms, and philosophies, serves as a powerful catalyst for innovation and creativity, driving economic growth and enhancing the nation's global appeal. The country's rich heritage, encompassing ancient monuments, historical sites, and living traditions, attracts tourists from across the globe, generating revenue and creating employment opportunities in the hospitality, tourism, and related sectors. Furthermore, India's diverse culinary traditions, music, dance, and theatre forms provide a fertile ground for creative industries, fostering innovation in areas such as fashion, design, and entertainment. By promoting and preserving its cultural heritage, India can not only strengthen its national identity but also unlock its economic potential. Moreover, India's diverse philosophical traditions, encompassing Hinduism, Buddhism, Jainism, and Sikhism, offer valuable insights into sustainable living, ethical business practices, and social harmony.

These principles can guide the nation's development trajectory, ensuring that economic growth is aligned with environmental sustainability and social justice. Embracing a pluralistic approach to education, incorporating diverse perspectives and knowledge systems, can foster critical thinking, creativity, and problem-solving skills among students, preparing them to address the challenges of a rapidly changing world. By celebrating and leveraging its cultural diversity, India can foster a vibrant and innovative economy, promote sustainable development, and enhance its global standing. This holistic approach ensures that progress is not only measured in economic terms but also in terms of social well-being, cultural enrichment, and environmental sustainability.

Effective governance and inclusive policies are crucial for harnessing the benefits of unity in diversity and ensuring that all citizens have a voice in shaping the nation's development trajectory. Decentralization of power, empowering local communities to participate in decision-making processes, is essential for addressing the unique needs and aspirations of diverse regions and social groups. Promoting transparency and accountability in governance, ensuring that public resources are used efficiently and effectively, is crucial for building trust and fostering social cohesion. Furthermore, inclusive policies that address historical injustices and promote social equity are necessary for creating a level playing field for all citizens. This includes affirmative action policies, land reforms, and access to education and healthcare for marginalized communities. Strengthening democratic institutions, protecting freedom of speech and expression, and ensuring the rule of law are essential for safeguarding the rights of all citizens and promoting a culture of tolerance and respect for diversity. Moreover, promoting inter-community dialogue and conflict resolution mechanisms is crucial for preventing and managing social tensions, fostering a sense of shared citizenship and national identity. Investing in education and awareness programs that promote understanding and appreciation of India's diverse cultures and traditions can help to combat prejudice and discrimination. By fostering effective governance and inclusive policies, India can create an environment where all citizens feel valued, respected, and empowered to contribute to the nation's progress. This participatory approach ensures that development is not only economically sustainable but also socially just and politically inclusive, strengthening the foundations of 'Vikasit Bharat'. This commitment to inclusivity and good governance will pave the way for a more prosperous and harmonious future for all Indians.

Technological advancements, when strategically deployed, can bridge divides and accelerate inclusive development across India's diverse landscape. Digital connectivity, expanding access to internet and mobile technologies, can empower remote and marginalized communities, providing them with access to information, education, healthcare, and economic opportunities. E-governance initiatives, leveraging technology to deliver public services efficiently and transparently, can reduce corruption and improve citizen engagement. Furthermore, technology can be used to promote skill development and entrepreneurship, providing individuals with the tools and resources they need to succeed in the digital economy. For instance, online learning platforms can offer affordable and accessible education to students in remote areas, while e-commerce platforms can connect artisans and small businesses with wider markets. Moreover, technology can play a crucial role in promoting sustainable agriculture, providing farmers with access to weather information, market prices, and best practices. However, it is important to address the digital divide, ensuring that all citizens have equal access to technology and the skills needed to use it effectively. This requires investing in digital infrastructure, promoting digital literacy, and developing content that is relevant and accessible to diverse communities. Furthermore, it is important to address concerns about data privacy and security, ensuring that citizens' personal information is protected. By harnessing the power of technology responsibly and inclusively, India can accelerate its journey towards 'Vikasit Bharat', bridging divides and empowering all citizens to participate in the digital economy. This strategic integration of technology will foster innovation, improve efficiency, and enhance the quality of life for all Indians.

Environmental sustainability is inextricably linked to India's development aspirations, requiring a holistic approach that respects the ecological diversity of the nation and promotes climate resilience. India's diverse ecosystems, ranging from the Himalayas to the coastal regions, are vulnerable to the impacts of climate change, including rising sea levels, extreme weather events, and biodiversity loss. Protecting these ecosystems is crucial for ensuring the long-term well-being of communities that depend on them for their livelihoods and cultural survival. Promoting sustainable agriculture practices, such as organic farming and water conservation, can help to reduce greenhouse gas emissions and enhance food security. Investing in renewable energy sources, such as solar and wind power, can reduce India's dependence on fossil fuels and mitigate climate change. Furthermore, promoting sustainable urban development, including green buildings, public transportation, and waste management, can help to reduce pollution and improve the quality of life in cities. It is important to involve local communities in environmental conservation efforts, recognizing their traditional knowledge and empowering them to manage natural resources sustainably. This requires promoting participatory decision-making processes, providing access to information and resources, and ensuring that communities benefit from conservation efforts. Moreover, it is important to integrate environmental considerations into all aspects of development planning, ensuring that economic growth is aligned with environmental sustainability. By prioritizing environmental sustainability, India can not only protect its natural resources but also enhance its resilience to climate change and promote a more equitable and prosperous future for all. This commitment to environmental stewardship will ensure that 'Vikasit Bharat' is not only economically advanced but also ecologically responsible.

The path to 'Vikasit Bharat' is undeniably intertwined with the celebration and strategic utilization of India's inherent unity in diversity. This journey necessitates a paradigm shift, moving away from homogenization and embracing the unique strengths and potential of each community, region, and individual. By fostering inclusive policies, promoting effective governance, and leveraging technological advancements, India can unlock its full potential and achieve sustainable and equitable development. Recognizing the value of diverse knowledge systems, cultural traditions, and entrepreneurial spirit is crucial for driving innovation and creating a vibrant economy. Furthermore, prioritizing environmental sustainability and promoting climate resilience are essential for ensuring the long-term well-being of the nation and its citizens. The vision of 'Vikasit Bharat' is not merely about economic growth; it is about creating a society where all citizens have equal opportunities to thrive, where cultural diversity is celebrated, and where the environment is protected for future generations. This requires a collective effort, involving the government, civil society, the private sector, and individual citizens, all working together towards a shared goal. The challenges are significant, but the potential rewards are even greater. By embracing its unity in diversity, India can overcome these challenges and emerge as a global leader, demonstrating that development can be both inclusive and sustainable. The success of 'Vikasit Bharat' hinges on the ability to harness the collective wisdom, creativity, and resilience of its diverse population, creating a nation that is not only prosperous but also just, equitable, and harmonious. This holistic approach will ensure a brighter future for all Indians, leaving a legacy of progress and prosperity for generations to come.

India, a land of vibrant landscapes and ancient civilizations, has long been celebrated for its unparalleled diversity. This inherent pluralism, woven into the very fabric of the nation, is not by an understanding and appreciation of this diversity, can contribute to national development. Furthermore, it will analyze the challenges and opportunities inherent in fostering a truly inclusive society, where every citizen feels empowered to contribute their unique talents and perspectives to the natio

The source of strength and innovation. This principle, deeply rooted in India's historical and philosophical traditions, recognizes that a nation's progress is not achieved through homogenization but through the synergistic interaction of diverse perspectives, skills, and experiences. The * by fostering greater understanding and bonding between states and union territories through structured cultural exchanges. This initiative recognizes that regional disparities and a lack of awareness about different cultures can hinder national integration. By promoting reciprocal learning and appreciation, the program seeks to dismantle stereotypes, build bridges of understanding, and cultivate a sense of shared identity among citizens from diverse backgrounds. These exchanges encompass various aspects of culture, including language, literature, cuisine, festivals, arts, and music, allowing participants to experience firsthand the richness and variety of India's heritage. Moreover, the program encourages the sharing of best practices and innovative ideas across states, fostering a spirit of healthy competition and collaborative problem-solving. For instance, a state with a successful model for rural development can share its expertise with another state facing similar challenges, leading to more effective and sustainable solutions. This cross-pollination of ideas not only accelerates development but also strengthens the bonds of cooperation and mutual support between different regions. The initiative also leverages digital platforms to connect people from different parts of the country, facilitating virtual interactions and knowledge sharing. Through online forums, webinars, and social media campaigns, citizens can engage in discussions, exchange ideas, and learn about each other's cultures and traditions, further intercultural dialogue in schools and workplaces, encouraging participation in cultural events and festivals, and supporting initiatives that celebrate India's diversity. Individuals can also play a crucial role in challenging stereotypes and promoting inclusivity in their communities. By speaking out against discrimination and prejudice, and by actively promoting understanding and respect for different cultures, they can contribute to creating of India's diverse population, fostering a sense of shared ownership and responsibility for the nation's progress.

However. Socio-economic disparities, regional imbalances, and historical injustices can create barriers to inclusivity and hinder the full participation of all citizens in the nation's progress. Addressing these inequalities requires a multi-pronged approach that includes targeted interventions to uplift marginalized communities, promote equitable access to education and healthcare, and create economic opportunities for all. Furthermore, it is essential to foster a culture of tolerance and respect for diversity, where differences are celebrated rather than feared. This requires promoting critical thinking and media literacy to counter misinformation and stereotypes, as well as strengthening legal frameworks to protect the rights of minorities and vulnerable groups. The rise of divisive ideologies and hate speech poses a significant threat to social cohesion and national unity. Combating these forces requires a concerted effort from civil society organizations, educational institutions, and the government to promote dialogue, understanding, and empathy. It also requires holding individuals and organizations accountable for spreading hate and inciting violence. Overcoming these challenges is essential to unlock the full potential of India's diversity and create a truly inclusive and prosperous nation.

The encompasses economic integration and sustainable development. A unified and prosperous India requires a level playing field where all regions have the opportunity to thrive and contribute to the national economy. This necessitates addressing regional disparities in infrastructure, investment, and access to resources. Promoting balanced regional development can in renewable energy sources, and implementing effective environmental regulations. It also requires fostering a sense of environmental stewardship among citizens, encouraging them to adopt eco-friendly lifestyles and participate in conservation efforts. The concept also aligns with India's commitment to global cooperation and its role as a responsible global citizen. By promoting unity and harmony within its borders, India can serve as a model for other nations seeking to build inclusive and prosperous societies. India's rich cultural heritage and its commitment to democratic values make it a natural leader in promoting peace, understanding, and cooperation on the global

The role of individuals in fostering unity and driving national development cannot be overstated. Every citizen has a responsibility to contribute to the collective good and to promote the values of inclusivity, tolerance, and respect for diversity. This can take many forms, from engaging in community service and supporting local businesses to promoting intercultural dialogue and challenging discrimination. Education plays a crucial role in shaping individuals' attitudes and values. By promoting critical thinking, empathy, and a deeper understanding of India's history and culture, educational institutions can empower students to become active and engaged citizens. Furthermore, education can equip individuals with the skills and knowledge they need to contribute to the nation's economic development. The media also has a significant role to play in shaping public opinion and promoting national unity. By providing accurate and balanced coverage of events, and by highlighting the positive contributions of diverse communities, the media can help to counter stereotypes and promote understanding. However, it is also important for individuals to be critical consumers of media and to be aware of the potential for bias and misinformation. Technology can be a powerful tool for connecting people from different backgrounds and promoting intercultural dialogue. Social media platforms, online forums, and virtual exchange programs can facilitate communication and collaboration across geographical boundaries. However, it is also important to be aware of the potential for technology to be used to spread hate speech and misinformation. Individuals must use technology responsibly and ethically, and to promote positive and constructive online interactions. By embracing their roles as active and responsible citizens, individuals can contribute to building a stronger, more united, and more prosperous India.

The a holistic vision of national development that prioritizes social justice, environmental sustainability, and good governance. This requires a commitment to inclusive policies that address the needs of all citizens, regardless of their caste, religion, gender, or socio-economic background. It also requires strengthening democratic institutions, promoting transparency and accountability, and ensuring that all citizens have a voice in shaping the nation's future. Good governance is essential for creating an environment where businesses can thrive, innovation can flourish, and individuals can reach their full potential. This requires streamlining regulations, reducing corruption, and promoting a culture of ethical leadership. It also requires investing in infrastructure, education, and healthcare to values of unity, diversity, and inclusivity that have defined its identity for centuries. By embracing these values and working together towards a common vision, India can realize its full potential and become a truly incredible nation.

The but a civilizational imperative. It demands a continuous and conscious effort to nurture the bonds of unity, celebrate diversity, and empower individuals to contribute their best to the nation's progress. The challenges are significant, but the potential rewards are even greater. A truly united and inclusive India can unlock its vast human potential, drive innovation, and emerge as a global leader in the 21st century. Build consensus on key issues facing the nation. It also requires a commitment to upholding the values of justice, equality, and human dignity for all. The government plays a crucial role in creating an enabling environment for national integration and development. This includes implementing its full potential and emerge as a beacon of hope and inspiration for the world. It is a journey that requires the collective wisdom, strength, and resilience of all its people, working together to build a brighter future for generations to come.

As Bharat strides towards 2047, marking a century of independence, the concept of unity transcends mere political rhetoric, evolving into a critical imperative for realizing its envisioned potential. Unity, in its multifaceted dimensions – social, economic, cultural, and political – acts as the bedrock upon which a strong and prosperous nation can be built. It is the cohesive force that binds together a diverse populace, channeling their collective energies towards shared goals and aspirations. The journey to 2047 necessitates a re-evaluation of the existing fault lines that threaten to fragment the social fabric. These include persistent inequalities based on caste, religion, gender, and region, which hinder inclusive growth and perpetuate marginalization. Addressing these challenges requires a concerted effort to foster a sense of belonging and shared identity among all citizens, ensuring that the benefits of progress reach every corner of the nation. Furthermore, unity is indispensable for navigating the complex geopolitical landscape and asserting Bharat's rightful place on the global stage. A nation divided is vulnerable to external pressures and internal conflicts, undermining its ability to effectively pursue its strategic interests. Therefore, cultivating a strong sense of national purpose and solidarity is essential for safeguarding Bharat's sovereignty and promoting its influence in the world.

The socio-cultural dimension of unity is paramount in a nation as diverse as Bharat. The country's strength lies in its pluralism, a tapestry woven from myriad languages, religions, customs, and traditions. However, this very diversity can become a source of division if not carefully nurtured and managed. The rise of identity politics, often fueled by narrow sectarian interests, poses a significant threat to social cohesion. Such politics can exacerbate existing inequalities, create new fault lines, and undermine the spirit of mutual respect and understanding that is essential for a harmonious society. To counter these divisive forces, it is imperative to promote intercultural dialogue and exchange, fostering a deeper appreciation for the richness and complexity of Bharat's cultural heritage. Education plays a crucial role in this regard, by instilling in young minds a sense of national identity that transcends regional and parochial loyalties. The curriculum should emphasize the shared history and values that bind all Bharatiyas together, while also celebrating the unique contributions of each community to the national narrative. Furthermore, – the world is one family – should be embraced as a guiding principle, fostering a sense of global citizenship that complements national identity. This requires a commitment to inclusivity and tolerance, ensuring that all citizens feel valued and respected, regardless of their background or beliefs. By promoting a culture of empathy and understanding, Bharat can harness the power of its diversity to create a more vibrant and resilient society. This approach will not only strengthen the social fabric but also unlock the immense potential of its human capital, driving innovation and progress across all sectors.

Economic unity is equally crucial for Bharat's progress towards 2047. Regional disparities in economic development have long been a source of concern, with some states lagging far behind others in terms of income, infrastructure, and access to opportunities. These disparities not only create social tensions but also hinder overall economic growth, as they prevent the full utilization of the nation's resources and potential. To address this challenge, it is essential to promote balanced regional development, ensuring that all parts of the country benefit from economic progress. This requires targeted investments in infrastructure, education, and healthcare in less developed regions, as well as policies that encourage entrepreneurship and job creation. Furthermore, it is important to foster greater economic integration between states, removing barriers to trade and investment and promoting the free flow of goods, services, and people. The Goods and Services Tax (GST) was a significant step in this direction, creating a unified national market and reducing transaction costs. However, more needs to be done to streamline regulations and harmonize policies across states, creating a more level playing field for businesses and investors. In addition to regional disparities, income inequality within states is also a major concern. The gap between the rich and the poor has been widening in recent years, leading to social unrest and undermining social mobility. Addressing this issue requires a multi-pronged approach, including progressive taxation, social safety nets, and investments in education and skills development. By promoting inclusive growth and reducing economic disparities, Bharat can create a more prosperous and equitable society for all its citizens.

Political unity, characterized by a shared national vision and a commitment to democratic values, is indispensable for Bharat's success in the years leading up to 2047. A stable and effective government, accountable to its citizens and responsive to their needs, is essential for creating an environment conducive to economic growth, social progress, and national security. However, political polarization and fragmentation have become increasingly prevalent in recent years, threatening to undermine the foundations of Bharat's democracy. The rise of populism, the spread of misinformation, and the erosion of trust in institutions all pose significant challenges to political unity. To counter these trends, it is imperative to strengthen democratic institutions, promote civic education, and foster a culture of reasoned debate and dialogue. Political parties must prioritize the national interest over narrow partisan considerations, working together to find common ground on critical issues facing the country. Furthermore, it is essential to ensure that all citizens have a voice in the political process, regardless of their background or beliefs. This requires protecting the rights of minorities, promoting freedom of expression, and ensuring that elections are free and fair. In addition to internal political unity, Bharat must also project a united front on the global stage. A cohesive and consistent foreign policy, based on national interests and guided by principles of peace and cooperation, is essential for promoting Bharat's influence in the world and safeguarding its security. By strengthening its democratic institutions, promoting civic engagement, and projecting a united front on the global stage, Bharat can ensure that its political system remains resilient and responsive to the challenges of the 21st century. Therefore, a unified approach to governance and international relations is crucial for Bharat's continued progress and stability.

Technological unity, encompassing equitable access to technology and a unified approach to innovation, is increasingly vital as Bharat approaches 2047. The digital revolution presents both immense opportunities and potential risks. Bridging the digital divide, ensuring that all citizens have access to affordable internet and digital literacy, is crucial for inclusive growth. Unequal access to technology can exacerbate existing inequalities, creating a two-tiered society where some are left behind in the digital age. To address this challenge, it is essential to invest in digital infrastructure, promote digital literacy programs, and develop affordable technology solutions that cater to the needs of diverse communities. Furthermore, a unified approach to innovation is needed to harness the full potential of technology for economic and social development. This requires fostering collaboration between government, industry, and academia, creating an ecosystem that encourages innovation and entrepreneurship. Intellectual property rights must be protected, while also ensuring that the benefits of innovation are shared widely. In addition to promoting technological innovation, it is also important to address the ethical and social implications of new technologies. Issues such as data privacy, cybersecurity, and artificial intelligence require careful consideration and regulation to ensure that technology is used responsibly and ethically. By promoting technological unity, Bharat can leverage the power of technology to drive economic growth, improve public services, and empower its citizens. This unified approach will ensure that technology serves as a force for inclusion and progress, rather than exacerbating existing inequalities. Ultimately, a cohesive strategy for technological advancement is essential for Bharat to thrive in the 21st century.

Environmental unity, characterized by a shared commitment to sustainable development and a unified approach to environmental protection, is paramount for Bharat's long-term well-being as it approaches 2047. Climate change, pollution, and resource depletion pose significant threats to the country's environment and economy. Addressing these challenges requires a concerted effort from all stakeholders, including government, industry, and citizens. A unified approach to environmental protection is essential to ensure that policies are consistent, effective, and equitable. This requires strengthening environmental regulations, promoting sustainable practices in agriculture and industry, and investing in renewable energy sources. Furthermore, it is important to raise awareness among citizens about the importance of environmental protection and encourage them to adopt sustainable lifestyles. Education and public awareness campaigns can play a crucial role in fostering a sense of environmental responsibility. In addition to domestic efforts, Bharat must also play a leading role in international efforts to address climate change and protect the global environment. This requires working with other countries to develop and implement effective solutions, as well as advocating for a more equitable and sustainable global order. Protecting biodiversity and promoting sustainable use of natural resources are also crucial for environmental unity. This requires conserving forests, protecting wildlife habitats, and promoting sustainable fishing and farming practices. By adopting a unified approach to environmental protection, Bharat can ensure that its economic development is sustainable and that its natural resources are preserved for future generations. A collective dedication to environmental stewardship will safeguard Bharat's ecological heritage for the benefit of all.

As Bharat journeys towards 2047, the significance of unity in its various dimensions cannot be overstated. Social unity, built on mutual respect and understanding, is essential for harnessing the power of diversity and creating a harmonious society. Economic unity, characterized by balanced regional development and inclusive growth, is crucial for ensuring that all citizens benefit from progress. Political unity, founded on democratic values and a shared national vision, is indispensable for effective governance and national security. Technological unity, encompassing equitable access to technology and a unified approach to innovation, is vital for leveraging the power of technology for economic and social development. Environmental unity, characterized by a shared commitment to sustainable development and a unified approach to environmental protection, is paramount for long-term well-being. Achieving these forms of unity requires a concerted effort from all stakeholders, including government, civil society, and individual citizens. It requires a willingness to bridge divides, overcome prejudices, and work together towards common goals. Education, dialogue, and inclusive policies are essential tools for fostering unity and building a stronger, more prosperous Bharat. The challenges ahead are significant, but so too is the potential for progress. By embracing unity as a guiding principle, Bharat can overcome these challenges and realize its full potential as a global leader. The journey to 2047 is an opportunity to reaffirm the values of unity, diversity, and inclusivity that have always been at the heart of Bharat's identity. A nation united in purpose and action is well-equipped to navigate the complexities of the 21st century and build a brighter future for all its citizens. Therefore, a unified Bharat stands poised to achieve remarkable progress and secure.

India, a land of vibrant landscapes, diverse cultures, and a rich history, stands as a testament to the power of unity in diversity. This inherent characteristic has not only shaped the is not merely about economic or military might, but also about its ability to offer solutions rooted in its ancient wisdom, cultural values, and democratic principles. By embracing its diversity and promoting inclusivity, India can emerge as a beacon of hope and a model for harmonious coexistence in an increasingly interconnected world. The nation's ability to harness the potential of its diverse population, promote innovation, and foster a sense of shared purpose will be crucial in realizing its vision of becoming a global leader and a source of knowledge and inspiration for the world.

The representing the harmonious coexistence of various religions, languages, ethnicities, and traditions within a single nation. This unique characteristic has been a source of strength and resilience throughout India's history, enabling it to withstand external pressures and internal conflicts. The Indian Constitution, with achieved through various activities such as student exchange programs, cultural festivals, and joint projects that bring people together to collaborate and learn from each other. The program also leverages digital platforms to disseminate information about India's diverse culture and heritage, making it accessible to a wider audience. Through online portals, social media campaigns, and virtual events and preserving this diversity, the nation can achieve its full potential. India's commitment to inclusivity and cultural exchange will pave the way for a more harmonious and prosperous future.

India's journey towards becoming a Vishwaguru is intrinsically linked to its ability to leverage its diverse knowledge systems and traditional practices. The country has a rich heritage of ancient wisdom, scientific innovation, and artistic expression that can offer valuable insights to the world. From Ayurveda and Yoga to classical music and dance forms, India's cultural and intellectual traditions have the potential to address contemporary challenges and promote holistic well-being. By promoting these knowledge systems on a global scale, India can contribute to a more sustainable and equitable world order. The concept of Vishwaguru also entails India's role as a provider of solutions to global challenges. With its vast experience in addressing issues such as poverty, inequality, and environmental degradation, India can offer valuable lessons and innovative approaches to other nations. The country's success in implementing large-scale development programs, promoting inclusive growth, and harnessing renewable energy sources can serve as a model for other developing countries. Furthermore, India's commitment to multilateralism and its active participation in international forums demonstrate its willingness to work collaboratively with other nations to address global challenges. To realize its vision of becoming a Vishwaguru, India must invest in research and development, promote innovation, and foster a culture of entrepreneurship. The country needs to create an ecosystem that encourages creativity, supports startups, and facilitates the translation of knowledge into practical applications. By harnessing the potential of its young population and leveraging its technological capabilities, India can emerge as a hub of innovation and a source of cutting-edge solutions. Moreover, India must strengthen its educational institutions, promote skill development, and ensure that its workforce is equipped with the knowledge and skills required to meet the demands of the 21st century. India's ability to blend its traditional wisdom with modern technology will be crucial in shaping its role as a global leader and a source of knowledge and inspiration for the world. By embracing innovation, promoting inclusivity, and fostering a sense of shared purpose, India can pave the way for a more prosperous and sustainable future for all. The nation's commitment to knowledge sharing and global collaboration will solidify its position as a Vishwaguru, guiding the world towards a brighter tomorrow.

India's democratic values and its commitment to peaceful coexistence are essential components of its vision of becoming a Vishwaguru. As the world's largest democracy, India has a responsibility to uphold the principles of freedom, equality, and justice, both within its borders and on the global stage. The country's commitment to the rule of law, its independent judiciary, and its vibrant civil society serve as a model for other nations aspiring to build democratic institutions. Furthermore, India's foreign policy is guided by the principles of non-alignment, peaceful resolution of disputes, and respect for international law. The country has consistently advocated for a multilateral world order and has played a constructive role in promoting peace and stability in the region and beyond. India's commitment to diplomacy, dialogue, and cooperation makes it a valuable partner in addressing global challenges such as terrorism, climate change, and nuclear proliferation. To strengthen its position as a global leader, India must continue to promote democratic values, uphold human rights, and foster inclusive governance. The country needs to address issues such as poverty, inequality, and discrimination, and ensure that all its citizens have equal opportunities to participate in the political and economic life of the nation. By strengthening its democratic institutions and promoting social justice, India can enhance its credibility and influence on the global stage. India's unwavering commitment to democratic principles and peaceful coexistence will solidify its role as a Vishwaguru, guiding the world towards a more just and equitable future. The nation's ability to uphold these values will inspire other nations to embrace democracy and work towards a more peaceful and prosperous world.

The integration and promoting cultural exchange, thereby contributing to India's journey towards becoming a Vishwaguru This program aims to enhance interaction and promote mutual understanding between people of different states and union territories through the concept of pairing. Under this initiative, each state or union territory is paired with another, and they conduct activities to promote each other's language, culture, traditions, and tourism. This helps to break down stereotypes development outcomes. By learning from each other's experiences, states can adopt successful models and adapt them to their own contexts, thereby accelerating progress and promoting inclusive growth. Furthermore, the program promotes tourism and cultural exchange, which can boost local economies and create employment respected on the global stage. The program's success in fostering mutual understanding and collaboration will pave the way for a more harmonious and progressive India.

India's soft power, encompassing its cultural influence, values, and diplomatic initiatives, plays a crucial role in shaping its global image and advancing its interests. The country's rich cultural heritage, including its art, music, dance, literature, and philosophy, has a universal appeal and attracts people from all over the world. Indian cinema, particularly Bollywood, has a massive following in many countries and serves as a powerful tool for promoting Indian culture and values. Furthermore, India's spiritual traditions, such as Yoga and meditation, have gained immense popularity globally and contribute to the country's image as a source of peace and well-being. In addition to its cultural influence, India's values of democracy, pluralism, and non-violence resonate with people around the world and enhance its soft power. The country's commitment to peaceful resolution of disputes, its advocacy for human rights, and its support for international cooperation make it a respected and admired member of the global community. India's diplomatic initiatives, such as its humanitarian assistance programs, its peacekeeping operations, and its efforts to promote regional integration, further strengthen its soft power and enhance its influence on the world stage. To leverage its soft power effectively, India must invest in promoting its culture, values, and diplomatic initiatives through various channels. The country needs to support its artists, musicians, and filmmakers, and provide them with platforms to showcase their talent to the world. India also needs to strengthen its cultural diplomacy programs, promote educational exchanges, and encourage people-to-people interactions. Furthermore, India must use digital platforms and social media to disseminate information about its culture, values, and achievements, and engage with audiences around the world. By harnessing the power of its soft power, India can enhance its global image, build stronger relationships with other countries, and advance its interests in a peaceful and sustainable manner. India's ability to project its soft power effectively will be crucial in shaping its role as a Vishwaguru, guiding the world towards a more harmonious and prosperous future. The nation's commitment to cultural exchange, value-based diplomacy, and global cooperation will solidify its position as a source of inspiration and leadership for the world. By embracing its soft power assets, India can create a positive and lasting impact on the global stage.

India's journey towards becoming a Vishwaguru is a multifaceted endeavor that requires a holistic approach encompassing economic development, social progress, cultural promotion, and diplomatic engagement. The nation's inherent strength lies in its unity in diversity, which has enabled it to withstand challenges and emerge as a resilient and vibrant society. By embracing its diverse cultures, languages, and traditions, India can foster a sense of national identity and promote inclusivity, ensuring that all its citizens have equal opportunities to thrive. The Ek Bharat Shreshtha Bharat program serves as a valuable platform for promoting cultural exchange and mutual understanding between different states and union territories, strengthening the bonds of unity and fostering a shared sense of belonging. Furthermore, India's commitment to democratic values, peaceful coexistence, and multilateralism positions it as a responsible and respected member of the global community. The country's soft power, encompassing its cultural influence, values, and diplomatic initiatives, plays a crucial role in shaping its global image and advancing its interests. By leveraging its soft power assets, India can build stronger relationships with other countries, promote its culture and values, and contribute to a more peaceful and prosperous world. As India continues on its path towards becoming a Vishwaguru, it must remain committed to its core values of unity, diversity, democracy, and peaceful coexistence. The nation's ability to harness the potential of its diverse population, promote innovation, and foster a sense of shared purpose will be crucial in realizing its vision of becoming a global leader and a source of knowledge and inspiration for the world. India's journey towards becoming a Vishwaguru is not just about achieving economic or military might, but also about its ability.

Bharat Amritkaal, a period envisioned as a golden era of growth and prosperity. The very essence of this concept, the harmonious coexistence of myriad cultures, languages, religions, and traditions, has been a foundational pillar in shaping the nation's developmental trajectory. This inherent diversity, often perceived as a challenge, has paradoxically emerged as a source of strength, fostering innovation, resilience, and a unique socio-economic landscape. Its diverse threads into a cohesive national fabric. This intricate tapestry, rich in its variations, has provided a fertile ground for the cross-pollination of ideas, the development of indigenous solutions, and the creation of a vibrant and dynamic society. As Bharat embarks on its Amritkaal, the lessons learned from embracing its diversity become even more critical. The ability to leverage the unique skills, perspectives, and resources of its diverse population will be paramount in achieving sustainable and equitable development. This introduction will explore how the development of the concept of unity in diversity has paved the way for Bharat's progress, highlighting its role in fostering social cohesion, economic growth, and global leadership during this transformative period.

The concept of unity in diversity has profoundly shaped Bharat's socio-political landscape, fostering an environment conducive to inclusive development and national integration. The recognition and celebration of diverse cultural identities have played a crucial role in mitigating social conflicts and promoting harmony among different communities. This has been achieved through various mechanisms, including constitutional safeguards for minority rights, promotion of interfaith dialogue, and the preservation of cultural heritage. The Indian Constitution, with its emphasis on secularism, equality, and social justice, serves as a cornerstone in upholding the principles of unity in diversity. It guarantees fundamental rights to all citizens, irrespective of their religion, caste, gender, or ethnicity, ensuring that every individual has an equal opportunity to participate in the nation's progress. Furthermore, the promotion of regional languages and cultural expressions has helped to preserve the unique identities of different communities, while simultaneously fostering a sense of shared national identity. This approach has not only strengthened social cohesion but has also contributed to the enrichment of Bharat's cultural landscape. The emphasis on inclusive governance and participatory democracy has further empowered marginalized communities, enabling them to voice their concerns and contribute to policy-making processes. This has led to the development of more equitable and responsive policies that address the specific needs of diverse populations. Moreover, the celebration of festivals and cultural events from different regions has fostered a sense of mutual respect and understanding among people from different backgrounds. These events provide opportunities for cultural exchange and interaction, breaking down barriers and promoting a sense of shared identity. The success of Bharat's democratic experiment, despite its immense diversity, stands as a testament to the power of unity in diversity. The ability to accommodate diverse perspectives and interests within a single political framework has been instrumental in maintaining social stability and promoting economic growth. This inclusive approach has also enhanced Bharat's soft power on the global stage, making it a respected voice for peace, harmony, and international cooperation. The emphasis on social justice and equality has created a more inclusive and equitable society, laying the foundation for sustainable development and national progress.

Economically, Bharat's unity in diversity has fostered innovation and entrepreneurship by bringing together diverse skills, knowledge, and resources. Different regions of the country specialize in various industries and sectors, creating a complementary economic ecosystem. This specialization allows for efficient resource allocation, increased productivity, and enhanced competitiveness. The free flow of goods, services, and labor across state borders has further facilitated economic integration and growth. The diverse cultural backgrounds of entrepreneurs and business leaders have also contributed to the development of innovative products and services that cater to a wide range of consumer preferences. Moreover, the presence of diverse skill sets within the workforce has enabled Bharat to adapt to changing global market demands and capitalize on new opportunities. The promotion of regional economic development has also played a crucial role in reducing disparities and fostering inclusive growth. By investing in infrastructure, education, and healthcare in underdeveloped regions, the government has created opportunities for local communities to participate in the nation's economic progress. This has not only improved the living standards of marginalized populations but has also unlocked their potential to contribute to the overall economy. The success of Bharat's IT sector, for example, can be attributed to the diverse talent pool and the ability to leverage the skills of people from different regions and backgrounds. This has made Bharat a global hub for technology and innovation, attracting foreign investment and creating employment opportunities. The economic benefits of unity in diversity are evident in the country's sustained growth and its emergence as a major player in the global economy.

Bharat's diverse cultural heritage has significantly influenced its approach to global relations, positioning it as a bridge between different cultures and civilizations. The principles of non-alignment, peaceful coexistence, and multilateralism, deeply rooted in its history and philosophy, have guided its foreign policy. This has enabled Bharat to forge strong relationships with countries across the globe, irrespective of their political ideologies or economic systems. The country's commitment to promoting peace and stability in the region has also earned it respect and credibility on the international stage. Bharat's cultural diplomacy, which involves promoting its art, music, literature, and philosophy, has further enhanced its soft power and strengthened its ties with other nations. The celebration of Indian festivals and cultural events in different parts of the world has fostered cross-cultural understanding and appreciation. Moreover, the country's diaspora, spread across the globe, serves as a valuable asset in promoting its interests and building bridges between cultures. The contributions of the Indian diaspora to their host countries have been widely recognized, further enhancing Bharat's image as a responsible and peace-loving nation. Bharat's leadership in international organizations, such as the United Nations, has also been instrumental in shaping global policies and addressing pressing challenges, such as climate change, poverty, and terrorism. The country's commitment to sustainable development and its efforts to promote renewable energy have been widely appreciated. Furthermore, Bharat's humanitarian assistance during natural disasters and crises has demonstrated its compassion and solidarity with the global 'ommunity. The country's ability to leverage its diverse cultural heritage and its commitment to peaceful coexistence have made it a respected and influential player in global affairs. This approach has not only strengthened its relationships with other nations but has also contributed to a more peaceful and prosperous world. Bharat's unique position as a melting pot of cultures has enabled it to play a crucial role in fostering dialogue and understanding between different civilizations.

However, the path towards realizing the full potential of unity in diversity is not without its challenges. Social inequalities, regional disparities, and communal tensions continue to pose significant obstacles to inclusive development. Addressing these challenges requires a concerted effort from the government, civil society, and individuals. Strengthening social justice mechanisms, promoting inclusive education, and fostering interfaith dialogue are crucial steps in mitigating social inequalities and promoting harmony. Investing in infrastructure and economic development in underdeveloped regions is essential for reducing regional disparities and ensuring that all communities have an equal opportunity to participate in the nation's progress. Furthermore, promoting responsible media and combating misinformation are vital for preventing the spread of communal tensions and fostering a culture of tolerance and understanding. The government's commitment to Sabka Saath, Sabka Vikas, Sabka Vishwas (Together with all, Development for all, Trust of all) reflects its recognition of the importance of inclusive development and social harmony. This vision requires a multi-pronged approach that addresses the root causes of social inequalities and promotes a sense of shared national identity. Moreover, empowering local communities and promoting participatory governance are essential for ensuring that development initiatives are aligned with the needs and aspirations of the people. Overcoming these challenges and harnessing the full potential of unity in diversity will be crucial for Bharat to achieve its Amritkaal vision of a prosperous, inclusive, and sustainable future. The continued commitment to these principles will pave the way for a brighter and more equitable future for all citizens.

Looking ahead, Bharat's Amritkaal presents a unique opportunity to further strengthen the foundations of unity in diversity and leverage its potential for accelerated development. Embracing technological advancements, promoting sustainable practices, and fostering innovation will be crucial for achieving inclusive and sustainable growth. Investing in education and skill development is essential for equipping the workforce with the knowledge and skills needed to thrive in the 21st century. Promoting research and development in areas such as renewable energy, healthcare, and agriculture will drive innovation and create new economic opportunities. Furthermore, leveraging digital technologies to bridge the gap between urban and rural areas will promote inclusive growth and empower marginalized communities. The government's focus on digitalization, infrastructure development, and ease of doing business will create a conducive environment for investment and entrepreneurship. Promoting sustainable practices and adopting a circular economy approach will ensure that development is environmentally responsible and resource-efficient. Moreover, fostering a culture of innovation and entrepreneurship will encourage the development of indigenous solutions to local challenges. The Amritkaal vision also emphasizes the importance of good governance, transparency, and accountability. Strengthening institutions, promoting ethical practices, and ensuring citizen participation are crucial for building a strong and resilient nation. Furthermore, promoting social harmony and fostering a sense of shared national identity will be essential for maintaining social stability and promoting economic growth. The success of Bharat's Amritkaal will depend on its ability to harness the collective wisdom and energy of its diverse population. By embracing its unity in diversity and promoting inclusive development, Bharat can achieve its aspirations of becoming a global leader and a beacon of hope for the world. This journey requires a collective commitment to building a nation where every citizen has the opportunity to thrive and contribute to the nation's progress.

The journey of Bharat towards its Amritkaal is inextricably linked to its ability to nurture and celebrate its unity in diversity. This inherent characteristic has not only shaped its socio-political landscape but has also fueled its economic growth and enhanced its global standing. The ability to accommodate diverse perspectives, foster innovation, and promote peaceful coexistence has been instrumental in the nation's progress. As Bharat moves forward, it is imperative to address the challenges that continue to impede the full realization of its potential. Social inequalities, regional disparities, and communal tensions must be tackled head-on through inclusive policies, equitable resource allocation, and proactive measures to promote harmony. The Amritkaal vision requires a collective commitment to building a nation where every citizen has the opportunity to thrive, contribute, and feel a sense of belonging. Embracing technological advancements, promoting sustainable practices, and fostering innovation will be crucial for achieving inclusive and sustainable growth. Investing in education, skill development, and research will empower the workforce and drive economic progress. Furthermore, strengthening governance, promoting transparency, and ensuring citizen participation will build a strong and resilient nation. Bharat's unique position as a melting pot of cultures and its commitment to peaceful coexistence have positioned it as a bridge between different civilizations. By leveraging its soft power and promoting multilateralism, Bharat can play a leading role in shaping a more peaceful and prosperous world. The continued emphasis on unity in diversity will undoubtedly pave the way for Bharat to achieve its Amritkaal aspirations and emerge as a global leader, inspiring other nations with its inclusive and sustainable development model.

In an increasingly interconnected world, the concept of unity in diversity stands as a cornerstone for peaceful coexistence and societal progress. It acknowledges and celebrates the differences in cultures, beliefs, and backgrounds, while simultaneously emphasizing the shared values and common humanity that bind us together. The youth, as the inheritors of this globalized world, possess a unique capacity to champion this ideal. Their energy, open-mindedness, and technological fluency position them as potential pioneers in fostering understanding and collaboration across diverse communities. The traditional structures and prejudices that have historically hindered unity are often less ingrained in younger generations. They are more likely to embrace new perspectives, challenge existing norms, and leverage digital platforms to connect with individuals from different walks of life. This inherent adaptability and willingness to engage with the unfamiliar make them powerful agents of change. Furthermore, the youth are not merely passive recipients of cultural exchange; they are active creators and shapers of it. Through music, art, social media, and various forms of creative expression, they can bridge cultural divides, promote empathy, and build a more inclusive and harmonious society. Their role in promoting unity in diversity is not just desirable, but essential for building a sustainable and equitable future for all. The following discussion will explore the specific ways in which the youth can effectively contribute to this vital cause.

One of the most impactful ways the youth can champion unity in diversity is through active engagement in intercultural dialogue and exchange programs. These initiatives provide platforms for young people from different backgrounds to interact, share their experiences, and learn from one another. By participating in such programs, the youth can break down stereotypes, challenge preconceived notions, and develop a deeper understanding of diverse cultures and perspectives. This direct exposure fosters empathy and promotes a sense of shared humanity, which are crucial for building bridges across cultural divides. Moreover, the youth can leverage their digital fluency to facilitate intercultural dialogue on a global scale. Social media platforms, online forums, and virtual exchange programs offer unprecedented opportunities for young people to connect with peers from around the world. By engaging in respectful and constructive conversations online, they can share their own cultural heritage, learn about the traditions and customs of others, and address misunderstandings or misconceptions that may exist. This digital diplomacy can play a significant role in fostering cross-cultural understanding and promoting tolerance. Furthermore, the youth can actively seek out opportunities to learn new languages and immerse themselves in different cultures. Language proficiency is not only a valuable skill in today's globalized world, but it also opens doors to deeper cultural understanding and appreciation. By learning a new language, young people can gain insights into the values, beliefs, and perspectives of another culture, which can help them to communicate more effectively and build stronger relationships with people from diverse backgrounds. Immersion experiences, such as studying abroad or volunteering in a different country, can further enhance this cultural understanding and promote empathy. In addition to participating in formal exchange programs, the youth can also create their own initiatives to promote intercultural dialogue and understanding within their local communities. This could involve organizing cultural festivals, hosting international students, or volunteering with organizations that serve diverse populations. By taking proactive steps to engage with people from different backgrounds, the youth can create a more inclusive and welcoming environment for all. These proactive engagements will help to foster a more interconnected and understanding global community.

Another crucial role for the youth in fostering unity in diversity lies in their capacity to challenge discrimination and promote inclusivity. Young people are often more attuned to issues of social justice and equality, and they are more likely to speak out against prejudice and discrimination in all its forms. By actively challenging discriminatory attitudes and behaviors, the youth can create a more equitable and inclusive society for everyone. This can involve speaking out against racism, sexism, homophobia, and other forms of prejudice, both online and offline. It can also involve supporting policies and initiatives that promote equality and opportunity for all members of society. Furthermore, the youth can play a vital role in promoting inclusivity within their schools, workplaces, and communities. This can involve advocating for diversity and inclusion programs, creating safe spaces for marginalized groups, and challenging discriminatory practices. By taking proactive steps to create a more inclusive environment, the youth can help to ensure that everyone feels valued, respected, and empowered. Moreover, the youth can leverage their creativity and artistic talents to raise awareness about issues of discrimination and promote understanding and empathy. Through music, art, film, and other forms of creative expression, they can challenge stereotypes, share stories of marginalized communities, and inspire others to take action. This creative activism can be a powerful tool for promoting social change and building a more just and equitable world. By actively challenging discrimination and promoting inclusivity, the youth can pave the way for a more unified and harmonious society where everyone has the opportunity to thrive. This proactive stance is essential for building a future where diversity is celebrated and all individuals are treated with dignity and respect.

The youth's engagement in promoting unity in diversity extends significantly into the realm of education and awareness campaigns. They can actively participate in designing and implementing educational programs that highlight the importance of cultural understanding, tolerance, and respect for differences. By taking on this role, they contribute to shaping a more informed and empathetic society. This involvement can manifest in various forms, such as developing workshops, seminars, and online resources that explore different cultures, religions, and perspectives. These initiatives can be tailored to different age groups and educational settings, ensuring that the message of unity in diversity reaches a wide audience. Furthermore, the youth can leverage their digital skills to create engaging and informative content for social media platforms. Short videos, infographics, and interactive quizzes can be used to raise awareness about cultural diversity and challenge stereotypes. By using creative and accessible formats, they can effectively communicate complex ideas and inspire others to learn more. In addition to formal educational programs, the youth can also organize community events that celebrate cultural diversity. These events can feature music, dance, food, and art from different cultures, providing opportunities for people to come together and learn about one another in a fun and engaging way. By creating these spaces for intercultural exchange, the youth can foster a sense of community and belonging. Moreover, the youth can advocate for the inclusion of diverse perspectives in school curricula and textbooks. They can work with educators and policymakers to ensure that students are exposed to a wide range of voices and experiences, promoting a more comprehensive and nuanced understanding of the world. By actively shaping the educational landscape, the youth can help to create a more inclusive and equitable society for future generations. These educational endeavors will help to cultivate a society that values diversity and promotes understanding among all its members.

Young people can also contribute significantly to unity in diversity by actively participating in collaborative projects that address global challenges. Many of the most pressing issues facing the world today, such as climate change, poverty, and inequality, require collaborative solutions that transcend cultural and national boundaries. By working together on these projects, the youth can build bridges across diverse communities and promote a sense of shared responsibility for the future. This collaboration can take many forms, from participating in international volunteer programs to launching social enterprises that address local needs. By working alongside people from different backgrounds, the youth can learn valuable skills, broaden their perspectives, and develop a deeper understanding of the challenges facing the world. Furthermore, the youth can leverage technology to facilitate collaboration on a global scale. Online platforms and communication tools can be used to connect young people from different countries and cultures, enabling them to share ideas, resources, and expertise. By working together virtually, they can overcome geographical barriers and create innovative solutions to global problems. In addition to participating in existing projects, the youth can also create their own initiatives to promote collaboration and address global challenges. This could involve launching a crowdfunding campaign to support a community development project, organizing a virtual conference to discuss climate change solutions, or creating a social media campaign to raise awareness about human rights issues. By taking proactive steps to address global challenges, the youth can demonstrate their commitment to unity in diversity and inspire others to take action. These collaborative efforts will help to build a more sustainable and equitable world for all.

Finally, the youth can serve as powerful role models and advocates for unity in diversity within their own communities and beyond. By embodying the values of tolerance, respect, and understanding in their daily lives, they can inspire others to embrace diversity and challenge prejudice. This involves actively promoting inclusivity in their schools, workplaces, and social circles, and speaking out against discrimination whenever they encounter it. Furthermore, the youth can use their voices to advocate for policies and initiatives that promote unity in diversity at the local, national, and international levels. This could involve writing letters to elected officials, participating in peaceful protests, or supporting organizations that work to advance social justice and equality. By actively engaging in the political process, they can help to shape a more inclusive and equitable society for all. In addition to their advocacy efforts, the youth can also share their own stories and experiences to promote understanding and empathy. By sharing their personal narratives, they can help to humanize complex issues and challenge stereotypes. This storytelling can take many forms, from writing blog posts and creating videos to giving public speeches and participating in community events. Moreover, the youth can mentor and support younger generations, helping them to develop the skills and values they need to become effective advocates for unity in diversity. By serving as positive role models, they can inspire younger people to embrace diversity and challenge prejudice in their own lives. This intergenerational mentorship can play a crucial role in building a more inclusive and harmonious society for future generations. By serving as role models and advocates, the youth can inspire a broader movement towards unity and understanding, creating a ripple effect that extends far beyond their immediate communities. This dedication to promoting inclusivity will help to build a more just and equitable world for all.

The youth possess an unparalleled capacity to be pioneers in supporting unity in diversity. Their inherent adaptability, technological fluency, and commitment to social justice position them as powerful agents of change in an increasingly interconnected world. Through active engagement in intercultural dialogue, challenging discrimination, promoting education and awareness, participating in collaborative projects, and serving as role models and advocates, they can effectively bridge cultural divides and build a more inclusive and harmonious society. The potential for the youth to shape a future where diversity is celebrated and all individuals are treated with dignity and respect is immense. Their proactive involvement in fostering understanding and collaboration across diverse communities is not merely desirable, but essential for building a sustainable and equitable future for all. By embracing their role as pioneers, the youth can inspire a broader movement towards unity and understanding, creating a ripple effect that extends far beyond their immediate communities. The journey towards unity in diversity is an ongoing process that requires continuous effort and commitment. However, by harnessing the energy, creativity, and passion of the youth, we can pave the way for a more just and equitable world where everyone has the opportunity to thrive. The responsibility lies with all of us to support and empower the youth in their efforts to promote unity in diversity, ensuring that their voices are heard and their contributions are valued. This collective effort will help to build a future where differences are celebrated and common humanity is embraced.

India, a land of staggering diversity, presents a unique tapestry woven from myriad languages, religions, castes, customs, and traditions. This inherent heterogeneity, while a source of immense cultural richness, also-state is built, requiring continuous and concerted efforts to nurture and sustain it. Intercultural programs and government ministries play a crucial role in fostering this unity by actively promoting understanding, respect, and appreciation for the diverse cultures that constitute India. These initiatives aim to bridge cultural divides, dismantle stereotypes, and cultivate a sense of shared identity and belonging among citizens from different backgrounds. By facilitating dialogue, exchange, and collaboration across cultural boundaries, they contribute to building a more inclusive and harmonious society.

A primary function of intercultural programs and relevant ministries is to promote cultural awareness and understanding through education and outreach initiatives. These programs often target schools, colleges, and community centers, aiming to instill in individuals, from a young age, an appreciation for India's diverse heritage. Curricula are designed to incorporate the history, literature, arts, and traditions of various cultural groups, fostering empathy and respect among students. Workshops, seminars, and cultural festivals are organized to provide platforms for interaction and exchange, allowing people from different backgrounds to learn about each other's customs, beliefs, and values. The Ministry of Culture, for instance, plays a pivotal role in preserving and promoting India's cultural heritage through various schemes and initiatives. It supports the documentation, conservation, and dissemination of traditional art forms, music, dance, and theater. The Ministry also establishes and maintains cultural institutions, such as museums, libraries, and archives, which serve as repositories of knowledge and centers for cultural learning. Furthermore, it organizes national and international cultural events to showcase India's diversity and promote intercultural dialogue. Beyond formal education, intercultural programs also leverage media and technology to reach a wider audience. Television programs, radio broadcasts, and online platforms are used to disseminate information about different cultures, challenge stereotypes, and promote positive narratives about diversity. Social media campaigns are employed to raise awareness about cultural issues and encourage intercultural understanding. These efforts aim to create a more informed and tolerant public, capable of appreciating and celebrating India's multicultural identity. Moreover, the government supports research and documentation of various cultural practices, providing valuable resources for understanding and preserving India's intangible heritage. These educational and outreach efforts are crucial in laying the foundation for a more inclusive and harmonious society, where diversity is recognized as a strength and a source of national pride. By fostering a deeper understanding of India's cultural mosaic, these initiatives contribute to breaking down barriers and building bridges between communities. This proactive engagement with cultural education cultivates a society that values inclusivity and mutual respect.

Another significant aspect of intercultural programs and ministerial efforts is the promotion of social inclusion and equality. Recognizing that certain marginalized communities face systemic discrimination and exclusion, these initiatives aim to address historical injustices and create a more equitable society.

Affirmative action policies, such as reservations in education and employment, are implemented to provide opportunities for disadvantaged groups and promote their representation in various sectors. The Ministry of Social Justice and Empowerment plays a crucial role in formulating and implementing policies and programs for the welfare of Scheduled Castes, Scheduled Tribes, Other Backward Classes, and persons with disabilities. These initiatives include scholarships, vocational training programs, and financial assistance for self-employment. Furthermore, the government promotes inter-caste and inter-religious marriages to break down social barriers and foster greater integration. Incentive schemes are often offered to couples who choose to marry outside their caste or religion, encouraging greater social mixing and challenging traditional norms. Intercultural programs also work to address issues of discrimination and prejudice through awareness campaigns and legal interventions. They provide support to victims of discrimination and advocate for stronger laws and policies to protect the rights of marginalized communities. These efforts are essential in creating a society where everyone has equal opportunities and is treated with dignity and respect. By actively promoting social inclusion and equality, these initiatives contribute to building a more just and harmonious India. This commitment to equity strengthens the fabric of unity within the nation's diverse population.

Furthermore, intercultural programs and government ministries actively foster dialogue and collaboration between different cultural groups to promote mutual understanding and resolve conflicts. Recognizing that misunderstandings and stereotypes can often lead to tensions and divisions, these initiatives create platforms for people from diverse backgrounds to come together, share their perspectives, and build relationships. Community-based dialogues, interfaith meetings, and joint cultural projects are organized to facilitate communication and cooperation. The Ministry of Minority Affairs plays a vital role in promoting the welfare of religious minorities and fostering interfaith harmony. It supports initiatives that encourage dialogue and understanding between different religious communities, and it provides assistance to minority educational institutions and organizations. The government also promotes the celebration of festivals and cultural events of different communities, providing opportunities for people from all backgrounds to participate and learn about each other's traditions. These celebrations serve as a reminder of India's shared heritage and promote a sense of national unity. In conflict-prone areas, intercultural programs work to promote reconciliation and peacebuilding. They facilitate dialogue between conflicting groups, address grievances, and promote healing and forgiveness. These initiatives often involve community leaders, religious figures, and civil society organizations, who work together to build trust and restore social harmony. Moreover, the government supports initiatives that promote cultural exchange and tourism, encouraging people from different parts of the country to visit and experience each other's cultures. These exchanges help to break down stereotypes and promote a greater appreciation for India's diversity. By fostering dialogue and collaboration, these initiatives contribute to building a more cohesive and harmonious society, where differences are celebrated and conflicts are resolved peacefully. This emphasis on communication and cooperation strengthens the bonds of unity within India's diverse population.

Despite the significant efforts made by intercultural programs and government ministries, challenges remain in achieving true unity in diversity in India. Deep-rooted social inequalities, historical prejudices, and political polarization continue to pose obstacles to social cohesion. Discrimination based on caste, religion, gender, and ethnicity persists in various forms, hindering the full participation of marginalized communities in society. The rise of religious fundamentalism and intolerance also threatens India's secular fabric and undermines efforts to promote interfaith harmony. The spread of misinformation and hate speech through social media further exacerbates these challenges, creating divisions and fueling conflicts. Moreover, the implementation of intercultural programs often faces bureaucratic hurdles, resource constraints, and a lack of coordination between different agencies. The effectiveness of these programs is also hampered by a lack of monitoring and evaluation, making it difficult to assess their impact and identify areas for improvement. Addressing these challenges requires a multi-pronged approach that involves strengthening legal frameworks, promoting inclusive education, empowering marginalized communities, and fostering critical thinking and media literacy. It also requires greater political will and commitment to promoting social justice and equality. Furthermore, it is essential to engage civil society organizations, community leaders, and religious figures in the effort to build a more inclusive and harmonious society. Overcoming these obstacles is crucial to realizing the full potential of India's diversity and building a truly united nation. A sustained and concerted effort is needed to address these persistent issues and ensure that all citizens have the opportunity to thrive and contribute to India's progress.

To enhance the effectiveness of intercultural programs and ministerial efforts, several key strategies can be adopted. Firstly, there is a need for greater emphasis on grassroots initiatives that directly engage with communities and address their specific needs and concerns. This requires decentralizing program implementation and empowering local organizations to design and deliver culturally relevant interventions. Secondly, it is crucial to strengthen monitoring and evaluation mechanisms to assess the impact of intercultural programs and identify areas for improvement. This involves developing clear indicators of success, collecting data on program outcomes, and conducting regular evaluations to inform program design and implementation. Thirdly, there is a need for greater collaboration and coordination between different government agencies, civil society organizations, and the private sector. This requires establishing platforms for dialogue and information sharing, and developing joint strategies to address common challenges. Fourthly, it is essential to invest in research and documentation to better understand the dynamics of cultural diversity in India and identify effective approaches to promoting unity and social cohesion. This involves supporting academic research, conducting surveys and studies, and documenting best practices in intercultural relations. Fifthly, there is a need for greater emphasis on promoting critical thinking and media literacy to counter misinformation and hate speech. This involves educating citizens about the importance of verifying information, identifying biases, and engaging in constructive dialogue. Finally, it is crucial to foster a culture of empathy, respect, and understanding through education, awareness campaigns, and cultural exchanges. By adopting these strategies, intercultural programs and government ministries can more effectively promote unity in diversity in India and build a more inclusive and harmonious society. These improvements will lead to a more profound and lasting impact on the nation's social fabric.

The intercultural programs and government ministries play a vital role in fostering unity in diversity in India. Through education, outreach, social inclusion initiatives, and the promotion of dialogue and collaboration, these efforts contribute to building a more inclusive and harmonious society. While significant progress has been made, challenges remain in addressing deep-rooted social inequalities, historical prejudices, and the rise of intolerance. To enhance the effectiveness of these programs, it is essential to prioritize grassroots initiatives, strengthen monitoring and evaluation mechanisms, foster collaboration between stakeholders, invest in research and documentation, promote critical thinking and media literacy, and cultivate a culture of empathy and respect. By adopting these strategies, India can more effectively leverage its cultural diversity as a source of strength and build a truly united nation. The journey towards unity in diversity is an ongoing process that requires sustained commitment and effort from all stakeholders. It demands a willingness to confront uncomfortable truths, challenge ingrained biases, and embrace the richness and complexity of India's cultural mosaic. Ultimately, the success of this endeavor depends on the collective will of the Indian people to build a society where everyone feels valued, respected, and empowered to participate fully in the nation's progress. Only then can India truly realize its potential as a beacon of unity in a diverse world, demonstrating that differences can be a source of strength and that a shared sense of belonging can transcend cultural boundaries. The continued dedication to these principles will shape a brighter and more unified future for India.

India, a land celebrated for its breathtaking tapestry of cultures, languages, religions, and traditions, stands at a pivotal juncture in its history. The nation's aspiration to ascend as a global leader and project its unique identity on the world stage hinges significantly on its ability to harness the power of unity in diversity. This concept, far from being a mere slogan, represents a fundamental principle that underpins India's strength and potential. The very essence of India lies in its multifaceted nature, where ancient customs coexist with modern aspirations, and regional variations contribute to a vibrant national identity. However, this diversity also presents challenges, as differences can sometimes lead to divisions and conflicts. To truly thrive and assume a leadership role in the international arena, India must actively cultivate a sense of shared purpose and collective responsibility among its diverse population. Unity in diversity implies recognizing, respecting, and celebrating the differences that enrich the Indian experience, while simultaneously fostering a sense of belonging and common identity. It requires transcending narrow parochial interests and embracing a broader vision of national progress, where every citizen feels valued and empowered to contribute their unique talents and perspectives. This essay will explore the critical importance of unity in diversity for India's global leadership aspirations, examining how it can strengthen the nation's social fabric, promote economic growth, and enhance its international standing.

A cohesive and Inclusive society, built upon the foundation of unity in diversity, is essential for India to unlock its full economic potential and emerge as a global economic powerhouse. When diverse communities coexist harmoniously, it fosters an environment conducive to innovation, entrepreneurship, and economic growth. Different cultures and perspectives bring unique ideas and approaches to problem-solving, leading to more creative and effective solutions. Moreover, a united society is more likely to attract foreign investment and partnerships, as it signals stability and a conducive business environment. The Indian diaspora, spread across the globe, serves as a powerful example of how diversity can be a source of strength. These communities, while maintaining their distinct cultural identities, have made significant contributions to their adopted countries and have also acted as bridges between India and the rest of the world. Their success demonstrates the potential of a diverse and inclusive society to generate economic opportunities and enhance India's global influence. Furthermore, unity in diversity promotes social harmony and reduces the likelihood of conflicts, which can disrupt economic activity and hinder development. When people feel a sense of belonging and shared identity, they are more likely to cooperate and work together towards common goals. This is particularly important in a country like India, where social divisions based on caste, religion, and language have historically posed challenges to economic progress. By fostering a culture of inclusivity and mutual respect, India can create a more stable and prosperous society, attracting both domestic and foreign investment. A unified approach also allows for the efficient implementation of government policies and programs aimed at promoting economic development. When diverse communities are united, it is easier to build consensus and garner support for initiatives that benefit the entire nation. This is crucial for addressing challenges such as poverty, inequality, and unemployment, which require a coordinated and collaborative effort from all stakeholders. A strong sense of national unity also enhances India's bargaining power in international trade negotiations and economic partnerships. When India speaks with one voice, it is more likely to secure favorable terms and agreements that benefit its economy and its citizens. Therefore, fostering unity in diversity is not just a social imperative but also an economic necessity for India to achieve its global leadership aspirations. A society that embraces its diversity and works together towards common goals is better positioned to achieve sustainable and inclusive economic growth. This collective strength will undoubtedly pave the way for India.

Beyond economic benefits, unity in diversity is crucial for strengthening India's social fabric and promoting a more inclusive and equitable society. When people from different backgrounds come together, they learn from each other, broaden their perspectives, and develop a greater understanding and appreciation for different cultures and ways of life. This fosters empathy, tolerance, and mutual respect, which are essential for building a harmonious and cohesive society. In a diverse country like India, where social divisions have historically been a source of conflict and inequality, promoting unity is particularly important. By actively working to bridge divides and create a sense of shared identity, India can overcome these challenges and build a more just and equitable society for all its citizens. Education plays a vital role in fostering unity in diversity. By incorporating diverse perspectives and experiences into the curriculum, schools can help students develop a deeper understanding of India's rich cultural heritage and promote a sense of national pride. Furthermore, education can equip students with the critical thinking skills necessary to challenge stereotypes and prejudices and to engage in constructive dialogue across differences. Government policies and programs also play a crucial role in promoting social inclusion and reducing inequality. By implementing affirmative action policies, providing equal access to education and healthcare, and promoting economic opportunities for marginalized communities, the government can help to level the playing field and create a more just society. Civil society organizations and community groups also play a vital role in promoting unity in diversity. By organizing cultural events, interfaith dialogues, and community service projects, these organizations can bring people from different backgrounds together and foster a sense of shared purpose. A society that values diversity and promotes inclusion is more likely to be resilient and adaptable in the face of challenges. When people feel a sense of belonging and shared identity, they are more likely to support each other and work together to overcome adversity. This collective resilience is essential for India to navigate the complex challenges of the 21st century and emerge as a global leader. This unified strength will undoubtedly enhance India's global standing and influence.

On the international stage, a united and diverse India can project a powerful and compelling image, enhancing its diplomatic influence and soft power. A country that embraces its diversity and promotes inclusivity is more likely to be seen as a responsible and trustworthy global actor. This can lead to stronger relationships with other countries and greater influence in international organizations. India's rich cultural heritage, a product of its diversity, is a valuable asset in its diplomatic efforts. By showcasing its diverse traditions, art forms, and philosophies, India can attract cultural exchange, promote tourism, and foster goodwill among nations. This cultural diplomacy can help to build bridges of understanding and cooperation, strengthening India's relationships with countries around the world. Furthermore, a united India is better positioned to advocate for its interests on the global stage. When India speaks with one voice, it is more likely to be heard and respected by other nations. This is particularly important in addressing global challenges such as climate change, terrorism, and poverty, which require a coordinated and collaborative effort from all countries. India's commitment to democracy and pluralism, values that are deeply rooted in its diverse society, also enhances its international standing. By upholding these values at home, India can serve as a model for other countries and promote democracy and human rights around the world. A united and diverse India is also better equipped to contribute to global peace and security. With its diverse population and its long history of peaceful coexistence, India can play a constructive role in resolving conflicts and promoting reconciliation in other parts of the world. This commitment to peace and stability further enhances India's reputation as a responsible global leader. This unified approach will undoubtedly solidify India's position as a respected and influential member of the international community.

However, achieving unity in diversity is not without its challenges. India faces numerous obstacles, including persistent social inequalities, regional disparities, and the rise of divisive ideologies. Overcoming these challenges requires a concerted effort from all stakeholders, including the government, civil society, and individual citizens. One of the key challenges is addressing the historical injustices and inequalities that continue to affect marginalized communities. Caste-based discrimination, religious intolerance, and gender inequality remain significant problems in India, hindering social cohesion and undermining the principles of unity in diversity. To address these issues, the government must implement policies that promote social justice, equality, and inclusion. This includes strengthening affirmative action programs, promoting access to education and healthcare for marginalized communities, and enacting laws that protect the rights of all citizens. Another challenge is managing regional disparities and ensuring that all parts of India benefit from economic growth and development. Uneven development can lead to resentment and alienation, undermining national unity. To address this, the government must invest in infrastructure, education, and healthcare in underdeveloped regions and promote policies that create economic opportunities for all. The rise of divisive ideologies, such as religious fundamentalism and ethnic nationalism, also poses a threat to unity in diversity. These ideologies seek to divide society along religious or ethnic lines, undermining the principles of tolerance, mutual respect, and shared citizenship. To counter these ideologies, it is essential to promote critical thinking, interfaith dialogue, and a sense of shared national identity. Education, media, and civil society organizations all have a role to play in promoting these values. Furthermore, it is important to address the root causes of social unrest and conflict, such as poverty, inequality, and discrimination. By creating a more just and equitable society, India can reduce the appeal of divisive ideologies and promote social harmony. Overcoming these challenges requires a long-term commitment and a willingness to confront difficult issues. However, the rewards of achieving unity in diversity are immense, paving the way for a stronger, more prosperous, and more influential India on the global stage. This collective effort will undoubtedly solidify India's position as a beacon of unity and diversity in the world.

To effectively leverage unity in diversity, India must invest in strengthening its democratic institutions and promoting good governance. A robust and accountable democracy is essential for ensuring that the voices of all citizens are heard and that their rights are protected. This requires strengthening the rule of law, promoting transparency and accountability in government, and ensuring that elections are free and fair. Furthermore, it is crucial to promote decentralization and empower local governments to address the specific needs of their communities. This allows for more responsive and effective governance and promotes a sense of ownership and participation among citizens. Good governance also requires investing in education, healthcare, and other essential services. By providing equal access to these services, the government can help to level the playing field and create a more just and equitable society. This, in turn, strengthens social cohesion and promotes unity in diversity. Moreover, it is important to foster a culture of civic engagement and encourage citizens to participate in the democratic process. This can be achieved through education, awareness campaigns, and by creating opportunities for citizens to engage with their elected representatives. A vibrant civil society also plays a crucial role in promoting good governance and holding the government accountable. By supporting civil society organizations and promoting freedom of expression, India can strengthen its democratic institutions and ensure that the government is responsive to the needs of its citizens. Ultimately, good governance is essential for creating an environment where unity in diversity can thrive. When citizens trust their government and feel that their voices are heard, they are more likely to embrace their shared national identity and work together towards common goals. This collaborative spirit will undoubtedly propel India towards its aspirations of global leadership.

In essence, the path to India's global leadership and impactful representation lies inextricably linked to its ability to nurture and celebrate unity in diversity. It is not merely a philosophical ideal but a pragmatic necessity for a nation aspiring to play a significant role on the world stage. By embracing its multifaceted identity, India can unlock its full economic potential, strengthen its social fabric, and enhance its international standing. The journey towards achieving this unity requires a multi-pronged approach, encompassing economic empowerment, social inclusion, and good governance. Addressing historical injustices, promoting equality, and fostering a sense of shared citizenship are crucial steps in building a cohesive and harmonious society. Investing in education, healthcare, and infrastructure, particularly in underdeveloped regions, is essential for ensuring that all citizens have the opportunity to thrive and contribute to the nation's progress. Furthermore, safeguarding democratic institutions, promoting transparency and accountability, and fostering civic engagement are vital for creating an environment where unity in diversity can flourish. The challenges are undeniable, but the potential rewards are immense. A united and diverse India can serve as a beacon of hope and inspiration for the world, demonstrating that different cultures and communities can coexist peacefully and productively. By embracing its unique identity and leveraging its collective strength, India can confidently assert its leadership on the global stage, advocating for its interests and contributing to a more just and equitable world order. The future of India as a global leader hinges on its ability to harness the power of its diversity, transforming it from a potential source of division into a wellspring of strength and innovation. This transformation will undoubtedly pave the way for a brighter and more prosperous future for India and the world.

India, a nation celebrated for its unparalleled diversity, stands at a pivotal juncture in its journey towards becoming a powerful vision for national progress that resonates deeply with the country's unique socio-cultural fabric. This mantra, championed as a cornerstone of contemporary Indian governance, seeks to harness the collective strength of its 1.4 billion citizens, transcending the divides of caste, creed, religion, region, and gender The concept acknowledges that sustainable and equitable development cannot be achieved without the active participation and unwavering trust of every segment of society. It represents a paradigm shift from top-down approaches to a more participatory and collaborative model of governance, where every individual feels empowered to contribute to the nation's growth story. This introduction will explore how this inclusive philosophy is being implemented across various sectors, examining its impact on fostering unity in diversity and paving the way for a more prosperous and harmonious India. It will delve into the challenges and opportunities that lie ahead as the nation strives to translate this ambitious vision into tangible realities, ensuring that the fruits of progress are shared by all, leaving no one behind.

The partnerships in driving India's development agenda. This collaborative spirit is evident in various government initiatives that actively seek the participation of diverse stakeholders, including state governments, local communities, civil society organizations, and the private sector. For instance, the

Goods and Services Tax (GST) regime, a landmark tax reform, was implemented through extensive consultations and consensus-building among all states, demonstrating a commitment to cooperative federalism. Similarly, to international collaborations, with India actively engaging with global partners to address shared challenges such as climate change, poverty, and terrorism. By fostering a culture of inclusivity and collaboration, India is leveraging its diverse strengths to achieve common goals and build a more resilient programs aimed at empowering the poor and disadvantaged, such as the Pradhan Mantri Jan Dhan Yojana (National Mission for Financial Inclusion), which has brought millions of unbanked individuals Into the formal banking system, and the Pradhan Mantri Awas Yojana (Housing for All), which aims to provide affordable housing to the urban and rural poor. Furthermore, initiatives like the National Health Mission and the Sarva Shiksha Abhiyan (Education for All) are focused on improving access to quality healthcare and education, respectively, particularly in underserved areas. By prioritizing inclusive growth, India is striving to create a more just and equitable society where everyone has the opportunity to thrive and reach their full potential, thereby reducing inequality and fostering social harmony.

The-building. It recognizes that the government alone cannot achieve the ambitious goals of a vibrant India and that the active participation of every citizen is crucial. This principle is reflected in various initiatives that encourage volunteerism, social entrepreneurship, and community involvement in development projects. For example, the Swachh Bharat Abhiyan (Clean India Mission) has mobilized millions of citizens to participate in cleanliness drives and promote sanitation, leading to significant improvements in public health and hygiene. Similarly, initiatives like the Beti Bachao, Beti Padhao (Save the Daughter, Educate the Daughter) campaign have raised awareness about gender equality and encouraged communities to support the education of girls. Furthermore, the government is promoting digital literacy and financial inclusion to empower citizens and enable them to participate more effectively in the economy and society. By fostering a sense of ownership and responsibility among citizens, India is harnessing the power of collective collective endeavor is essential for realizing the vision of a New India where every citizen is empowered to contribute to the nation's progress.

The concept need to create an envIronment where citizens feel confident in the fairness and integrity of the system. This involves promoting transparency, accountability, and responsiveness in government institutions, as well as ensuring that justice is accessible to all. The government has taken several steps to enhance transparency, such as the implementation of the Right to Information (RTI) Act, which empowers citizens to seek information from public authorities. Additionally, efforts are being made to streamline bureaucratic processes, reduce corruption, and improve service delivery through the use of technology. Initiatives like the Digital India program aim to transform India into a digitally empowered society and knowledge economy, enhancing transparency and efficiency in governance. Furthermore, the government is committed to protecting the rights of minorities and marginalized communities, ensuring that they have equal opportunities and are treated with dignity and respect. This includes promoting social harmony and interfaith dialogue, as well as taking strict action against those who incite violence or discrimination. By fostering a culture of trust and mutual respect, India can strengthen its social fabric and create a more inclusive and harmonious society. The government's commitment to good governance and social justice is essential for building a New India where every citizen feels safe, secure, and valued. By prioritizing transparency, accountability, and inclusivity, India can create a more just and equitable society where everyone has the opportunity to thrive and reach their full potential. The government's efforts to promote good governance and social justice are crucial for building a strong and united India, where every citizen feels a sense of belonging and ownership.

India's rich cultural heritage and its diverse traditions, languages, and religions are a source of strength and resilience. The concept recognizes the importance of preserving and promoting this diversity, while also fostering a sense of national unity and identity. The government has taken several initiatives to promote cultural exchange and understanding, such as the Ek Bharat Shreshtha Bharat (One India, Great India) program, which aims to enhance interaction and promote mutual understanding between people of different states and cultures. Additionally, efforts are being made to protect and preserve India's tangible and intangible cultural heritage, including its monuments, museums, and traditional arts and crafts. The government is also promoting the use of technology to showcase India's cultural diversity to the world, through initiatives like the Incredible India campaign and the promotion of cultural tourism. By celebrating its diversity and promoting cultural understanding, India can strengthen its social fabric and create a more inclusive and harmonious society. The government's commitment to preserving and promoting India's cultural heritage is essential for building a strong and united nation, where every citizen feels proud of their identity and heritage. By embracing its diversity and fostering a sense of national unity, India can create a vibrant and prosperous future for all its citizens.

While the concept has yielded positive results, several challenges remain in its effective implementation. One of the key challenges is ensuring that the benefits of development reach all sections of society, particularly the most vulnerable and marginalized. This requires addressing issues such as poverty, inequality, and social exclusion, as well as promoting inclusive growth and sustainable development. Another challenge is overcoming the barriers to effective participation and collaboration, such as lack of awareness, capacity constraints, and institutional bottlenecks. This requires strengthening local governance, promoting citizen engagement, and building trust between government and citizens. Furthermore, there is a need to address the challenges of corruption, inefficiency, and lack of accountability in government institutions, which can undermine public trust and hinder development efforts. This requires promoting transparency, good governance, and ethical leadership, as well as strengthening anti-corruption mechanisms and promoting citizen oversight. Additionally, there is a need to address the challenges of social fragmentation and polarization, which can threaten social harmony and undermine national unity. This requires promoting interfaith dialogue, cultural understanding, and social inclusion, as well as addressing the root causes of conflict and violence. Overcoming these challenges requires a concerted effort from all stakeholders, including government, civil society, and citizens, as well as a commitment to inclusive growth, good governance, and social justice. By addressing these challenges effectively, India can realize the full potential of the concept and build a more prosperous, equitable, and harmonious society for all its citizens.

India's journey towards a vibrant and inclusive future is intrinsically linked to the successful implementation of the concept. This philosophy, with its emphasis on collective effort, inclusive growth, and mutual trust, provides a powerful framework for addressing the complex challenges and opportunities that lie ahead. By fostering a sense of shared ownership and responsibility among all citizens, India can harness its diverse strengths and build a more resilient, prosperous, and harmonious society. The principles of collaboration, participation, and trust are not merely slogans but rather essential ingredients for achieving sustainable and equitable development. As India continues its transformation, it is crucial to remain committed to these principles, ensuring that the benefits of progress are shared by all and that no one is left behind. The path forward requires a concerted effort from all stakeholders, including government, civil society, and citizens, to overcome the challenges and realize the full potential of this transformative vision. By embracing inclusivity, promoting good governance, and fostering a culture of trust and mutual respect, India can pave the way for a brighter future, where every citizen has the opportunity to thrive and contribute to the nation's progress. The success of this endeavor will not only shape India's destiny but also serve as an inspiration for other nations striving to build more inclusive and equitable societies. India's commitment to this vision is a testament to its enduring spirit of unity in diversity and its unwavering belief in the power of collective action.

India stands at a pivotal juncture, embarking on its 'Amrit Kal', a 25-year journey towards the centenary of its independence. This era is envisioned as a period of unprecedented growth, innovation, and global leadership, deeply rooted in its rich cultural heritage and the strength of its diverse populace. The 'Panch Pran', or five resolves, articulated by the Prime Minister, serve as guiding principles to navigate this transformative phase, fostering a sense of collective purpose and national unity. These five resolves – a developed India, removing any trace of colonialism, staying connected to our roots, unity, and a sense of duty among citizens – are not merely abstract ideals but actionable strategies designed to propel India towards a brighter future. They acknowledge the nation's aspirations for economic prosperity and technological advancement, while simultaneously emphasizing the importance of decolonization, cultural preservation, and civic responsibility. The beauty of the Panch Pran lies in their inherent ability to resonate across India's diverse social, cultural, and linguistic landscape. They provide a common framework for citizens to contribute to the nation's progress, irrespective of their background or beliefs. By embracing these resolves, India can harness the power of its unity in diversity, transforming it from a demographic reality into a dynamic force for national development. The Amrit Kal, therefore, is not just a period of economic growth, but also a time for social cohesion, cultural resurgence, and the reaffirmation of India's unique identity on the global stage. The Panch Pran are the cornerstones upon which this vision is built, paving the way for a stronger, more unified, and prosperous India.

The 'irst 'Pran', the resolve for a 'Developed India', directly addresses the nation's aspirations for economic prosperity and improved quality of life for all its citizens. This ambition transcends mere economic growth; it encompasses holistic development, including advancements in infrastructure, technology, education, and healthcare. Achieving this requires a concerted effort from all sections of society, fostering a sense of shared ownership and collective responsibility. For instance, initiatives like 'Make in India' and 'Digital India' encourage innovation and entrepreneurship, creating opportunities for individuals from diverse backgrounds to contribute to the nation's economic progress. Furthermore, investments in education and skill development empower marginalized communities, enabling them to participate more fully in the workforce and improve their socio-economic standing. The pursuit of a developed India also necessitates bridging the gap between urban and rural areas, ensuring equitable access to resources and opportunities. This can be achieved through improved infrastructure, access to technology, and targeted development programs that address the specific needs of rural communities. By working together towards a common goal of economic prosperity and social progress, Indians from all walks of life can forge a stronger sense of national unity. This shared ambition provides a powerful platform for collaboration and mutual support, transcending social and cultural differences. The vision of a developed India, therefore, serves as a unifying force, bringing together diverse communities under a common banner of progress and prosperity. It is a call to action for every citizen to contribute their skills and talents to the nation's development, fostering a sense of collective purpose and national pride. This collective endeavor strengthens the fabric of Indian society, reinforcing the bonds of unity and mutual respect.

The second 'Pran', the removal of any trace of colonialism, speaks to the need to decolonize the Indian mindset and reclaim its cultural identity. This resolve goes beyond merely dismantling colonial-era structures; it calls for a critical examination of internalized biases and a conscious effort to promote indigenous knowledge systems, arts, and traditions. Colonialism left a lasting impact on Indian society, influencing its education system, legal framework, and even its perception of itself. Removing these traces requires a multi-pronged approach, including promoting Indian languages, literature, and art forms, and incorporating indigenous knowledge into the curriculum. This process of decolonization can be a powerful unifying force, as it encourages Indians to rediscover their shared cultural heritage and take pride in their unique identity. By celebrating its diverse traditions and artistic expressions, India can strengthen its cultural fabric and foster a sense of collective belonging. Furthermore, decolonization also involves challenging discriminatory practices and promoting social justice. Colonial rule often exacerbated existing social inequalities, and addressing these historical injustices is crucial for building a more equitable and inclusive society. This requires a commitment to affirmative action, promoting equal opportunities for marginalized communities, and challenging discriminatory attitudes and behaviors. The removal of colonial traces also extends to the economic sphere, promoting self-reliance and reducing dependence on foreign powers. This can be achieved through policies that support domestic industries, promote innovation, and encourage entrepreneurship. By building a strong and self-reliant economy, India can assert its independence and chart its own course on the global stage. Embracing this resolve allows India to reclaim its narrative, celebrate its cultural richness, and build a more just and equitable society, thereby strengthening the bonds of unity and national pride. It is a journey of self-discovery and empowerment, enabling India to realize its full potential as a global leader.

The third 'Pran', staying connected to our roots, emphasizes the importance of preserving and promoting India's rich cultural heritage and traditional values. This resolve recognizes that India's strength lies in its diversity, and that preserving this diversity is essential for maintaining social cohesion and national unity. India's cultural heritage is a tapestry woven from countless threads of different languages, religions, customs, and traditions. Staying connected to these roots means celebrating this diversity and ensuring that it is passed on to future generations. This can be achieved through promoting cultural exchange programs, supporting traditional arts and crafts, and incorporating cultural education into the curriculum. Furthermore, staying connected to our roots also means upholding traditional values such as respect for elders, compassion, and community service. These values are deeply ingrained in Indian culture and play a vital role in maintaining social harmony and promoting ethical behavior. By upholding these values, Indians can strengthen their communities and build a more just and equitable society. This resolve also encourages a deeper understanding of India's history and philosophy. By learning about the contributions of past generations, Indians can gain a greater appreciation for their cultural heritage and develop a stronger sense of national identity. This understanding can also help to bridge divides and promote mutual respect between different communities. Staying connected to our roots is not about clinging to the past, but about drawing strength and inspiration from it to build a better future. It is about celebrating India's diversity, upholding its values, and promoting a deeper understanding of its history and philosophy. This commitment to cultural preservation strengthens the bonds of unity and national pride, enabling India to navigate the challenges of the modern world while remaining true to its unique identity. It is a testament to the enduring power of India's cultural heritage.

The fourth 'Pran', unity, underscores the critical importance of national cohesion and harmony in a diverse society like India. This resolve calls for transcending differences of caste, religion, region, and language to foster a sense of shared identity and collective purpose. Unity does not imply uniformity; rather, it celebrates the richness and vibrancy that arise from India's diversity. It requires mutual respect, understanding, and a willingness to embrace different perspectives. Promoting dialogue and communication between different communities is essential for building bridges and fostering empathy. This can be achieved through initiatives that encourage interfaith dialogue, cultural exchange programs, and educational campaigns that promote tolerance and understanding. Furthermore, unity also requires addressing social and economic inequalities that can fuel division and resentment. Ensuring equal opportunities for all citizens, regardless of their background, is crucial for building a more just and equitable society. This includes providing access to quality education, healthcare, and employment opportunities for marginalized communities. Strengthening democratic institutions and promoting good governance are also essential for maintaining unity. A fair and transparent system of governance ensures that all citizens have a voice and that their concerns are addressed. This fosters trust in the government and strengthens the bonds of citizenship. The spirit of unity also extends to promoting national integration and a sense of shared identity. This can be achieved through celebrating national holidays, promoting national symbols, and encouraging participation in national events. These activities foster a sense of belonging and reinforce the idea that all Indians are part of a larger national community. Embracing this resolve strengthens the social fabric of the nation, enabling India to overcome challenges and achieve its full potential. It is a testament to the power of collective action and the enduring spirit of Indian nationhood.

The fifth 'Pran', a sense of duty among citizens, emphasizes the importance of civic responsibility and active participation in nation-building. This resolve calls for every Indian to contribute to the country's progress, not just through their professional endeavors, but also through their actions as responsible citizens. A sense of duty encompasses a wide range of responsibilities, including obeying the law, paying taxes, and participating in the democratic process. It also includes contributing to the well-being of the community through volunteer work, charitable giving, and acts of kindness. Promoting civic education is essential for fostering a sense of duty among citizens. This includes teaching young people about their rights and responsibilities, as well as the importance of participating in the democratic process. Civic education can also help to promote critical thinking and problem-solving skills, enabling citizens to make informed decisions about the issues facing their communities. Furthermore, a sense of duty also involves holding the government accountable and demanding transparency and good governance. Citizens have a responsibility to speak out against corruption and injustice and to advocate for policies that promote the common good. This requires active engagement in the political process and a willingness to hold elected officials accountable for their actions. The spirit of duty also extends to protecting the environment and promoting sustainable development. Citizens have a responsibility to conserve resources, reduce pollution, and protect biodiversity for future generations. This requires adopting sustainable lifestyles and advocating for policies that promote environmental protection. Embracing this resolve strengthens the foundation of Indian democracy and empowers citizens to shape the future of their nation. It is a testament to the power of individual action and the collective responsibility of all Indians to build a better future for themselves and for generations to come. This commitment to civic duty ensures the continued progress and prosperity of the nation.

The 'Panch Pran' represent a powerful framework for India's journey through the 'Amrit Kal', providing a roadmap for achieving holistic development while preserving its unique cultural identity and strengthening its social fabric. These five resolves are not isolated goals but interconnected principles that reinforce each other, creating a synergistic effect that amplifies their impact. By striving for a developed India, removing colonial vestiges, staying connected to its roots, fostering unity, and cultivating a sense of duty among its citizens, India can unlock its full potential and emerge as a global leader. The success of the 'Panch Pran' hinges on the active participation and commitment of every Indian. It requires a collective effort to embrace these resolves and translate them into concrete actions. This includes promoting innovation and entrepreneurship, preserving cultural heritage, fostering dialogue and understanding between different communities, and holding the government accountable. The 'Amrit Kal' is a period of immense opportunity for India, but it also presents significant challenges. By embracing the 'Panch Pran', India can navigate these challenges and build a brighter future for all its citizens. This journey requires a shared vision, a collective commitment, and a unwavering belief in the power of unity in diversity. As India moves forward on this path, it is essential to remember that the 'Panch Pran' are not just abstract ideals but actionable strategies that can transform the nation. By embracing these resolves, India can create a society that is prosperous, just, equitable, and united, a nation that truly reflects the aspirations of its people and the richness of its cultural heritage. The 'Panch Pran' serve as a guiding light, illuminating the.

The aspiration for a unified, strong, and prosperous nation, deeply rooted in its rich cultural heritage and committed to progress. Realizing this vision requires a multi-faceted approach, addressing both the tangible and intangible aspects of national development. It necessitates fostering a sense of matter of economic advancement or infrastructural development. It demands a fundamental shift in mindset, encouraging empathy, understanding, and mutual respect across diverse communities. It calls for celebrating the unique strengths of each region and leveraging them for the collective good. This involves promoting cultural exchange, fostering innovation, and ensuring equitable access to opportunities for all, regardless of their background or location. The future of Bharat hinges on its ability to harness the power of its human capital, promote sustainable development, and strengthen its democratic institutions.

At sense of national identity and unity, transcending regional, linguistic, and cultural differences. This requires a conscious and sustained effort to promote understanding and appreciation of India's diverse heritage. Education plays a pivotal role in this endeavor, serving as a powerful tool for instilling values of patriotism, tolerance, and inclusivity from a young age. Curricula should be designed to showcase the rich tapestry of Indian history, art, literature, and philosophy, highlighting the contributions of various regions and communities to the nation's collective identity. Furthermore, educational institutions should actively encourage intercultural dialogue and exchange programs, providing students with opportunities to interact with peers from different backgrounds and broaden their perspectives. Beyond formal education, cultural exchange programs, festivals, and media initiatives can play a significant role in promoting national integration. Encouraging the free flow of ideas, art, and cultural expressions across state borders can help break down stereotypes and foster a sense of shared belonging. The media, in particular, has a responsibility to portray India's diversity in a positive and nuanced manner, avoiding sensationalism and promoting responsible reporting that celebrates the nation's unity in diversity. Furthermore, promoting a common national narrative that emphasizes shared values and aspirations is crucial for building a cohesive national identity. This narrative should be inclusive and representative of all sections of society, acknowledging the contributions of marginalized communities and addressing historical injustices. It should also emphasize the importance of civic engagement and responsible citizenship, encouraging individuals to actively participate in the democratic process and contribute to the betterment of society. In addition to fostering a sense of national identity has its own distinct cultural heritage, economic strengths, and social traditions, and these should be nurtured and promoted as valuable assets to the nation as a whole. By encouraging inter-state cooperation and knowledge sharing, India can leverage the unique strengths of each region to drive overall national development. This can involve promoting tourism, facilitating trade and investment, and sharing best practices in areas such as agriculture, education, and healthcare. By fostering a spirit of healthy competition and collaboration, India can unlock its full potential and emerge as a global leader.

Equitable and inclusive growth is paramount for realizing the vision of a strong and prosperous India. This entails ensuring that the benefits of economic development reach all sections of society, particularly the marginalized and vulnerable. Addressing income inequality, promoting social justice, and creating equal opportunities for all are essential for building a truly inclusive nation. Investing in education, healthcare, and skill development is crucial for empowering individuals and enabling them to participate fully in the economy. Providing access to quality education and healthcare services, regardless of socioeconomic background, is essential for breaking the cycle of poverty and promoting social mobility. Skill development programs should be aligned with the needs of the industry, equipping individuals with the skills and knowledge necessary to secure gainful employment. Furthermore, promoting entrepreneurship and innovation can create new economic opportunities and drive inclusive growth. Supporting small and medium-sized enterprises (SMEs), which are major drivers of job creation, is essential for fostering a vibrant and inclusive economy. Creating a conducive environment for innovation, by promoting research and development, protecting intellectual property rights, and encouraging risk-taking, can unlock new sources of economic growth and create high-skilled jobs. A commitment to social justice and equality is fundamental for building a strong and united India.

Strengthening democratic institutions and promoting good governance are vital for ensuring accountability, transparency, and citizen participation in the development process. A robust and independent judiciary, a free and fair electoral system, and a vibrant civil society are essential pillars of a healthy democracy. Ensuring the independence and impartiality of the judiciary is crucial for upholding the rule of law and protecting the rights of citizens. Strengthening the electoral system, by promoting voter awareness, combating electoral malpractices, and ensuring the participation of all eligible voters, is essential for maintaining the integrity of the democratic process. A vibrant civil society, comprising non-governmental organizations, community-based organizations, and citizen groups, plays a crucial role in holding the government accountable, advocating for the rights of marginalized communities, and promoting citizen participation in decision-making. Promoting transparency and accountability in governance is essential for combating corruption and ensuring that public resources are used effectively. Implementing measures such as the Right to Information Act, promoting e-governance, and strengthening anti-corruption agencies can help enhance transparency and accountability in government operations. Furthermore, fostering a culture of ethical leadership and promoting integrity in public service are crucial for building trust in government and ensuring that public officials act in the best interests of the citizens. Empowering local governments and promoting decentralization can also enhance citizen participation and improve the delivery of public services. By devolving power and resources to local bodies, governments can ensure that decisions are made closer to the people and that public services are tailored to the specific needs of local communities. This can also promote greater accountability and responsiveness on the part of local officials. Active citizen participation in governance is essential for ensuring that government policies and programs are aligned with the needs and aspirations of the people.

Sustainable development is not merely an option but a necessity for ensuring a prosperous future for Bharat. Balancing economic growth with environmental protection and social equity is crucial for creating a sustainable and resilient society. Investing in renewable energy, promoting energy efficiency, and adopting sustainable agricultural practices are essential for mitigating climate change and protecting the environment. Promoting the use of renewable energy sources, such as solar, wind, and hydro power, can reduce India's dependence on fossil fuels and lower greenhouse gas emissions. Improving energy efficiency in buildings, transportation, and industry can also significantly reduce energy consumption and lower carbon footprint. Adopting sustainable agricultural practices, such as organic farming, water conservation, and soil management, can enhance agricultural productivity while minimizing environmental impact. Protecting natural resources, such as forests, water bodies, and biodiversity, is crucial for maintaining ecological balance and ensuring the long-term sustainability of the economy. Implementing strict environmental regulations, promoting afforestation, and conserving water resources can help protect India's natural heritage. Furthermore, promoting sustainable consumption and production patterns is essential for reducing waste and minimizing environmental pollution. Encouraging the use of eco-friendly products, promoting recycling and waste management, and adopting circular economy principles can help create a more sustainable and resource-efficient economy. A commitment to sustainable development is essential for ensuring a healthy planet and a prosperous future for generations to come.

Innovation and technological advancement are critical drivers of economic growth and social progress in the 21st century. Investing in research and development, promoting a culture of innovation, and fostering collaboration between academia, industry, and government are essential for building a knowledge-based economy. Increasing investment in research and development (R&D) is crucial for driving innovation and technological advancement. Governments should allocate sufficient resources to support basic and applied research in areas such as science, technology, engineering, and mathematics (STEM). Promoting a culture of innovation, by encouraging creativity, risk-taking, and experimentation, is essential for fostering a vibrant innovation ecosystem. This can involve providing incentives for innovation, supporting startups and entrepreneurs, and creating platforms for knowledge sharing and collaboration. Fostering collaboration between academia, industry, and government can accelerate the translation of research findings into practical applications and drive economic growth. This can involve establishing joint research projects, promoting technology transfer, and creating incubators and accelerators to support startups. Furthermore, promoting digital literacy and providing access to technology are essential for empowering individuals and bridging the digital divide. Investing in digital infrastructure, providing affordable internet access, and promoting digital literacy programs can help ensure that all citizens have the opportunity to participate in the digital economy. Embracing emerging technologies, such as artificial intelligence, blockchain, and the Internet of Things, can transform industries, improve productivity, and create new economic opportunities. However, it is important to address the ethical and social implications of these technologies and ensure that they are used responsibly and for the benefit of all. By embracing innovation and technological advancement, India can unlock its full potential and emerge as a global leader in the knowledge economy.

The journey towards realizing the vision of a unified, strong, and prosperous India requires a collective commitment from all stakeholders. It demands a shared understanding of the challenges and opportunities that lie ahead, and a willingness to work together to overcome obstacles and achieve common goals. The essentials for building a strong and prosperous India are multifaceted and interconnected. Fostering a sense of national unity, promoting equitable and inclusive growth, strengthening democratic institutions, embracing sustainable development, and driving innovation and technological advancement are all critical components of this vision. Achieving this vision requires a long-term perspective and a sustained effort. It requires investing in education, healthcare, and infrastructure, promoting good governance, and fostering a culture of innovation and entrepreneurship. It also requires addressing social inequalities, protecting the environment, and promoting peace and harmony. The future of India depends on its ability to harness the power of its human capital, leverage its diverse strengths, and build a society that is just, equitable, and sustainable. By embracing these essentials, India can realize its full potential and emerge as a global leader, contributing to a more peaceful, prosperous, and sustainable world. The path forward requires unwavering dedication, collaborative action, and a shared belief in the potential of India to achieve greatness.

S instrumental role in unifying a fragmented nation after independence. His birth anniversary serves as a India, Great India) is a fitting tribute. This initiative aims to enhance interaction and promote mutual understanding between people of different states and union territories, fostering a stronger the building blocks of a nation, and their commitment to understanding, appreciating, and celebrating the diversity of India is crucial. Their role extends beyond passive observation; it demands active engagement in promoting cultural exchange, fostering empathy, and breaking down stereotypes. By

The from diverse regions. Citizens can actively participate by embracing opportunities to learn about the traditions, languages, and histories of states different from their own. This can be achieved through various means, such as participating in cultural festivals, attending workshops on regional arts and crafts, or even learning a new language. Educational institutions can play a vital role by organizing exchange programs that allow students to experience life in different parts of the country, fostering a sense of shared identity and national pride. Furthermore, citizens can leverage technology and social media platforms to connect with individuals from other states, sharing their own cultural experiences and learning from others. By actively engaging in these exchanges, citizens can break down stereotypes and misconceptions that often arise from a lack of understanding. This increased awareness can lead to greater empathy and respect for different cultures, fostering a sense of unity in diversity. For instance, a student from Tamil Nadu participating in a cultural exchange of South India might not only learn about the region's history and architecture but also contribute to the local tourism industry. Similarly, a group of friends from West Bengal trekking in the Himalayas might discover the unique biodiversity and cultural traditions of the region, while also supporting local communities. Furthermore, citizens can play a crucial role in promoting the consumption of products and services from different states. By supporting local artisans, businesses, and entrepreneurs from across the country, citizens can contribute to economic integration and regional development. This can be achieved through various means, such as purchasing handicrafts, textiles, and food products from different states, or utilizing services offered by businesses from other regions. For instance, a consumer from Kerala purchasing a handloom saree from Uttar Pradesh might not only support the local weavers but also contribute to the preservation of traditional weaving techniques. Similarly, a business from Gujarat outsourcing its IT services to a company in Karnataka might foster economic collaboration and regional growth. Through active participation in cultural exchange, promotion

Another crucial aspect of citizen participation lies in promoting a sense of shared responsibility towards national progress. This involves actively engaging in civic duties, such as voting, paying taxes, and upholding the law. Citizens must also be vigilant in safeguarding the nation's resources and protecting its environment. By adopting sustainable practices, such as conserving water and energy, reducing waste, and promoting afforestation, citizens can contribute to a cleaner and greener India. Furthermore, citizens can play a vital role in promoting social harmony and inclusivity. This involves challenging discriminatory practices, promoting gender equality, and advocating for the rights of marginalized communities. By fostering a culture of respect and tolerance, citizens can create a more just and equitable society. For instance, citizens can actively participate in community initiatives that promote interfaith dialogue and understanding. Similarly, they can support organizations that work to empower women and girls, providing them with access to education, healthcare, and economic opportunities. By actively promoting social harmony and inclusivity, citizens can contribute to a stronger and more united India. Through responsible citizenship and active participation in nation-building, individuals can contribute to the realization of a truly great India.

Furthermore, citizens can contribute significantly by actively participating in governance and policy-making processes. This involves engaging with elected representatives, participating in public consultations, and providing feedback on government policies. By holding their leaders accountable and demanding transparency and good governance, citizens can ensure that the government is responsive to their needs and aspirations. Citizens can also leverage technology and social media platforms to voice their opinions and concerns, participate in online discussions, and mobilize support for important causes. For instance, citizens can use social media to raise awareness about issues such as corruption, environmental degradation, or social injustice. They can also participate in online petitions and campaigns to advocate for policy changes. Furthermore, citizens can play a vital role in promoting innovation and entrepreneurship. By supporting startups, investing in new technologies, and creating a conducive environment for innovation, citizens can contribute to economic growth and job creation. This involves fostering a culture of risk-taking, encouraging creativity, and providing access to funding and mentorship for aspiring entrepreneurs. For instance, citizens can invest in startups through crowdfunding platforms or angel investor networks. They can also participate in hackathons and innovation challenges to develop new solutions to pressing problems. Furthermore, citizens can play a crucial role in promoting education and skill development. By supporting schools and educational institutions, volunteering as teachers or mentors, and providing access to learning resources, citizens can contribute to a more educated and skilled workforce. This involves promoting literacy, numeracy, and critical thinking skills, as well as providing vocational training and skill development programs. For instance, citizens can volunteer as tutors or mentors for underprivileged students. They can also donate books and learning materials to schools and libraries. By actively participating in governance, promoting innovation, and supporting education, citizens can contribute to a more prosperous and equitable India. Citizens' active involvement in these areas will pave the way for a stronger and more unified nation.

In addition to these broader roles, citizens can also contribute to the Ek Bharat Shreshtha Bharat initiative by promoting cultural tourism and showcasing the unique heritage of their respective states. This involves actively participating in tourism promotion activities, such as organizing cultural events, creating informative content about local attractions, and providing hospitality to visitors from other states. By showcasing the rich cultural diversity of India, citizens can attract tourists from across the country and the world, boosting local economies and fostering cross-cultural understanding. Furthermore, citizens can play a vital role in preserving and promoting traditional arts and crafts. This involves supporting local artisans, purchasing their products, and promoting their work through online and offline platforms. By preserving traditional arts and crafts, citizens can safeguard India's cultural heritage and provide livelihoods for artisans and craftspeople. For instance, citizens can organize exhibitions and workshops to showcase traditional arts and crafts. They can also purchase handicrafts as gifts or souvenirs, supporting local artisans and promoting their work. By actively promoting cultural tourism and preserving traditional arts and crafts, citizens can contribute to a more vibrant and culturally rich India. The collective effort of citizens in these endeavors will undoubtedly strengthen the bonds of unity and celebrate the diverse tapestry of Indian culture.

Moreover, the success of Ek Bharat Shreshtha Bharat hinges on fostering a spirit of volunteerism and community service among citizens. This involves actively participating in initiatives that address social challenges, such as poverty, inequality, and environmental degradation. By volunteering their time, skills, and resources, citizens can make a tangible difference in the lives of others and contribute to a more just and equitable society. This can take many forms, from participating in clean-up drives and tree plantation campaigns to providing education and healthcare services to underprivileged communities. Furthermore, citizens can play a crucial role in promoting digital literacy and bridging the digital divide. This involves volunteering as digital literacy trainers, providing access to computers and internet connectivity, and creating online resources in local languages. By empowering citizens with digital skills, we can enable them to participate more fully in the digital economy and access information and opportunities online. For instance, citizens can volunteer as digital literacy trainers in their local communities, teaching basic computer skills to senior citizens or underprivileged youth. They can also donate computers and internet access to schools and libraries in underserved areas. Furthermore, citizens can play a vital role in promoting health and wellness. This involves adopting healthy lifestyles, participating in health awareness campaigns, and volunteering in healthcare facilities. By promoting health and wellness, we can reduce the burden of disease and improve the quality of life for all citizens. For instance, citizens can participate in yoga and meditation classes, promote healthy eating habits, and volunteer in blood donation camps. By fostering a spirit of volunteerism, promoting digital literacy, and supporting health and wellness, citizens can contribute to a more resilient and prosperous India. The dedication of citizens to these causes will undoubtedly strengthen the social fabric of the nation and promote a sense of collective responsibility.

In essence, the success of Ek Bharat Shreshtha Bharat, commemorating the birth anniversary of Sardar Vallabhbhai Patel, rests significantly on the active and conscious participation of its citizens. It is not merely a government initiative but a collective endeavor that requires the commitment and involvement of every individual. From promoting cultural exchange and fostering empathy to upholding civic duties and contributing to nation-building, citizens have a multifaceted role to play in realizing the vision of a united and prosperous India. By embracing diversity, promoting inclusivity, and actively engaging in governance and community service, citizens can contribute to a stronger and more vibrant nation. The spirit of Ek Bharat Shreshtha Bharat should permeate every aspect of our lives, guiding our actions and shaping our interactions with others. It is a call to action for every citizen to rise above narrow parochial interests and embrace a broader sense of national identity. By working together, we can build a nation that is not only economically prosperous but also socially just and culturally rich. As we commemorate the birth anniversary of Sardar Vallabhbhai Patel, let us rededicate ourselves to the ideals of unity, integrity, and service to the nation. Let us strive to create an India where every citizen feels a sense of belonging and pride, and where the diverse cultures and traditions of our country are celebrated and cherished. Through collective effort and unwavering commitment, we can transform the vision of Ek Bharat Shreshtha Bharat into a tangible reality.

In an increasingly interconnected world, the concept of global recognition has become paramount for individuals, organizations, and even nations seeking to amplify their impact and influence. Achieving such recognition necessitates a multifaceted approach, and at its core lies the strategic utilization of technology to foster solidarity. Solidarity, in this context, refers to the unity and cooperation among individuals or groups who share common interests, goals, or sympathies. Technology, with its unparalleled capacity to connect people across geographical boundaries and facilitate the rapid dissemination of information, serves as a powerful catalyst for building and sustaining this crucial solidarity. The ability to leverage technology for collective action and shared purpose is no longer a luxury but a necessity for those aspiring to be recognized on a global stage. From grassroots movements advocating for social change to international collaborations addressing pressing global challenges, technology empowers individuals and groups to transcend traditional limitations and forge meaningful connections with like-minded individuals worldwide. This introduction will explore the multifaceted ways in which technology facilitates solidarity and, consequently, enhances the prospects of achieving global recognition. It will delve into the mechanisms through which digital platforms, communication tools, and data-sharing initiatives contribute to building bridges, fostering understanding, and amplifying voices, ultimately paving the way for greater visibility and influence in the global arena.

Technology's role in fostering solidarity begins with its capacity to break down geographical barriers and connect individuals and groups who share common interests or face similar challenges, regardless of their physical location. Digital platforms, such as social media networks, online forums, and collaborative workspaces, provide virtual spaces where people from diverse backgrounds can come together to exchange ideas, share experiences, and coordinate actions. These platforms transcend traditional limitations of time and space, enabling real-time communication and collaboration on a global scale. For instance, activists fighting for human rights in different countries can use encrypted messaging apps to share information, organize protests, and mobilize support, while researchers working on climate change can collaborate on data analysis and modeling using cloud-based platforms. The power of technology to connect people is particularly evident in the rise of transnational social movements. These movements, which address issues that transcend national borders, such as climate change, economic inequality, and human rights, rely heavily on technology to mobilize support, coordinate actions, and amplify their voices. Social media platforms, in particular, have become essential tools for these movements, allowing them to bypass traditional media outlets and communicate directly with the public. The Arab Spring uprisings, for example, demonstrated the power of social media to facilitate collective action and challenge authoritarian regimes. Similarly, the global climate strike movement has used social media to mobilize millions of people around the world to demand action on climate change. Furthermore, technology facilitates the formation of online communities based on shared interests or identities. These communities provide a sense of belonging and support for individuals who may feel isolated or marginalized in their offline lives. Online forums, social media groups, and virtual support groups allow people to connect with others who understand their experiences and share their perspectives. These communities can be particularly important for individuals who face discrimination or stigma, such as LGBTQ+ individuals, people with disabilities, or members of minority groups. By providing a safe and supportive space for these individuals to connect and share their experiences, technology can help to build solidarity and empower them to advocate for their rights. Ultimately, technology's ability to connect people across geographical boundaries and facilitate the formation of online communities is essential for building solidarity and promoting collective action on a global scale, thereby increasing the chances of global recognition for shared causes.

Beyond simply connecting people, technology plays a crucial role in facilitating the rapid dissemination of information, which is essential for raising awareness about important issues and mobilizing support for collective action. Digital platforms provide a powerful means of sharing news, research, and personal stories, allowing individuals and organizations to reach a global audience with unprecedented speed and efficiency. Social media, in particular, has become a primary source of information for many people, and it can be used to quickly spread awareness about pressing issues, such as human rights abuses, environmental disasters, and social injustices. However, the rapid dissemination of information also presents challenges, such as the spread of misinformation and disinformation. It is therefore essential to develop strategies for combating fake news and promoting media literacy. Fact-checking organizations, for example, play a crucial role in verifying information and debunking false claims. Education programs can also help people to develop critical thinking skills and learn how to evaluate the credibility of sources. In addition to raising awareness, technology can also be used to mobilize support for collective action. Online petitions, crowdfunding campaigns, and social media activism can all be used to generate public pressure and influence decision-makers. Online petitions, for example, allow people to easily express their support for a particular cause and can be used to demonstrate the level of public concern about an issue. Crowdfunding campaigns can be used to raise money for important projects, such as disaster relief efforts or the development of new technologies. Social media activism can be used to organize protests, boycott campaigns, and other forms of collective action. By facilitating the rapid dissemination of information and providing tools for mobilizing support, technology empowers individuals and organizations to raise awareness, advocate for change, and ultimately gain recognition for their causes on a global scale.

Furthermore, technology enables the creation and sharing of data, which can be used to inform decision-making, track progress, and hold actors accountable. Open data initiatives, for example, make government data freely available to the public, allowing citizens to monitor government performance and identify areas where improvements are needed. Data visualization tools can be used to present complex data in an accessible and engaging way, making it easier for people to understand the issues and take action. In the context of global recognition, data can be used to demonstrate the impact of solidarity efforts and to track progress towards achieving shared goals. For example, data on poverty rates, access to education, and environmental indicators can be used to assess the effectiveness of development programs and to identify areas where more resources are needed. Data on human rights violations can be used to hold perpetrators accountable and to advocate for policy changes. Technology also facilitates the development of monitoring and evaluation systems, which can be used to track the progress of solidarity initiatives and to identify areas where adjustments are needed. These systems can collect data on a variety of indicators, such as the number of people reached by a program, the level of participation in activities, and the changes in attitudes and behaviors. The data collected can then be used to assess the impact of the initiative and to make recommendations for improvement. Moreover, blockchain technology offers new possibilities for enhancing transparency and accountability in solidarity efforts. Blockchain, a decentralized and immutable ledger, can be used to track the flow of funds, verify the authenticity of data, and ensure that resources are being used effectively. By providing a transparent and auditable record of transactions, blockchain can help to build trust and confidence in solidarity initiatives. Ultimately, the ability to create, share, and analyze data is essential for informing decision-making, tracking progress, and holding actors accountable, thereby strengthening solidarity and enhancing the prospects of achieving global recognition for collective efforts.

However, it is crucial to acknowledge that technology is not a panacea and that its use in fostering solidarity also presents challenges. The digital divide, for example, refers to the gap between those who have access to technology and those who do not. This divide can exacerbate existing inequalities and limit the ability of marginalized groups to participate in online communities and access information. Addressing the digital divide requires investments in infrastructure, education, and affordable access to technology. Another challenge is the potential for technology to be used for malicious purposes, such as spreading misinformation, inciting violence, and engaging in cyberbullying. It is therefore essential to develop strategies for mitigating these risks and promoting responsible use of technology. This includes educating people about online safety, developing tools for detecting and removing harmful content, and holding perpetrators accountable for their actions. Furthermore, concerns about data privacy and security must be addressed. As more and more data is collected and shared online, it is important to ensure that this data is protected from unauthorized access and misuse. This requires implementing strong data security measures, developing clear privacy policies, and empowering individuals to control their own data. In addition to these challenges, it is also important to recognize that technology is not a substitute for face-to-face interaction and that building strong relationships requires more than just online communication. While technology can facilitate communication and collaboration, it is essential to also invest in building trust and understanding through personal interactions. By addressing these challenges and promoting responsible use of technology, we can maximize its potential to foster solidarity and enhance the prospects of achieving global recognition for shared causes.

Looking ahead, the potential for technology to foster solidarity and enhance global recognition is likely to grow even further. Emerging technologies, such as artificial intelligence (AI), virtual reality (VR), and blockchain, offer new opportunities for connecting people, sharing information, and mobilizing support. AI, for example, can be used to personalize learning experiences, translate languages in real-time, and identify patterns in data that can inform decision-making. VR can be used to create immersive experiences that allow people to empathize with others and understand different perspectives. Blockchain can be used to create secure and transparent systems for tracking donations, verifying identities, and managing supply chains. The metaverse, a shared virtual world, also holds promise for fostering solidarity by creating new spaces for people to connect, collaborate, and build communities. In the metaverse, people can interact with each other in real-time, regardless of their physical location. They can also create and share content, participate in virtual events, and build virtual economies. However, it is important to ensure that the metaverse is developed in a way that is inclusive and accessible to all. This requires addressing issues such as digital literacy, affordability, and accessibility for people with disabilities. Furthermore, it is essential to develop ethical guidelines for the use of these technologies to ensure that they are used in a way that promotes human rights, social justice, and environmental sustainability. This includes addressing issues such as bias in AI algorithms, the spread of misinformation in VR environments, and the environmental impact of blockchain technology. As technology continues to evolve, it is crucial to remain mindful of its potential benefits and risks and to develop strategies for maximizing its positive impact on society. By embracing innovation while also addressing ethical concerns, we can harness the power of technology to build a more connected, equitable, and sustainable world, thereby amplifying the potential for global recognition of shared values and goals.

In summation, the strategic utilization of technology stands as an indispensable tool for fostering solidarity and achieving global recognition in our increasingly interconnected world. Technology's capacity to transcend geographical barriers, facilitate the rapid dissemination of information, and enable data-driven decision-making empowers individuals, organizations, and movements to amplify their impact and influence on a global scale. However, it is crucial to acknowledge that technology is not a panacea and that its use also presents challenges, such as the digital divide, the spread of misinformation, and concerns about data privacy. Addressing these challenges requires a multifaceted approach that includes investments in infrastructure, education, and ethical guidelines. Looking ahead, emerging technologies such as AI, VR, and blockchain offer new opportunities for fostering solidarity and enhancing global recognition. However, it is essential to ensure that these technologies are developed and used in a way that is inclusive, equitable, and sustainable. Ultimately, the successful integration of technology into solidarity efforts requires a holistic approach that combines technological innovation with ethical considerations, social responsibility, and a commitment to building strong relationships. By embracing this approach, we can harness the power of technology to create a more connected, just, and sustainable world, where shared values and goals are recognized and celebrated on a global stage.

1. "Incredible Bharat is not just a dream; it's the heartbeat of our collective vision for a Viksit Bharat—where innovation meets tradition."

2. "To build a Viksit Bharat, we must plant the seeds of passion and purpose in the soil of Incredible Bharat, nurturing growth for generations to come."

3. "Viksit Bharat calls for a symphony of voices—from mountains to metropolises—each note echoing the incredible spirit of its people."

4. "An Incredible Bharat is the canvas; a Viksit Bharat is the masterpiece. Let us paint our future with the hues of hope and hard work."

5. "As we envision a Viksit Bharat, let the incredible stories of our past fuel the fire of our future, illuminating the path ahead."

6. "Incredible Bharat ignites the flame of possibility, transforming into a Viksit Bharat where every dream can take flight."

7. "Let us weave the fabric of a Viksit Bharat with the threads of unity, creativity, and the incredible tapestry of our diverse heritage."

8. "Viksit Bharat is a promise—the incredible journey from aspirations to achievements, where each step forward lights the way for all."

1. "In the heart of every Bharatiya beats the promise of a Viksit Bharat—where innovation meets heritage on the path of progress."

2. "A Viksit Bharat is not just a dream; it's a collective vision sculpted by our unity, diversity, and unwavering spirit."

3. "As the dawn breaks on a Viksit Bharat, let each sunrise inspire us to weave the threads of tradition with the fabric of modernity."

4. "Incredible Bharat: where every step towards development is powered by the wheels of creativity, compassion, and collaboration."

5. "In our quest for a Viksit Bharat, let us empower the unheard, uplift the unseen, and celebrate the beauty of our shared journey."

6. "When bold ideas meet a rich legacy, Incredible Bharat becomes not just a vision, but a vibrant reality—shaping tomorrow, today."

7. "Dream, strive, and build—Incredible Bharat is a mosaic of aspirations turned into a thriving Viksit Bharat for generations to come."

8. "The spirit of Incredible Bharat fuels our movement towards a Viksit Bharat, reminding us that our greatest achievements lie ahead."

1. "Incredible Bharat thrives as a tapestry of identities, woven together by the golden thread of unity — for in our diversity lies our strength."

2. "Viksit Bharat envisions a nation where every voice sings in harmony; it is our differences that compose the symphony of progress."

3. "As we journey towards a developed Bharat, let our hearts beat in unison, for unity in diversity is the true essence of our vibrant land."

4. "Within the mosaic of cultures lies the true pulse of Bharat; each piece adds brilliance to our collective dream of growth and unity."

5. "Incredible Bharat lays the groundwork for Viksit Bharat, where every step forward honors the roots of diversity that ground our shared future."

6. "Let us embrace Bharat's myriad colors—not as separate shades but as a magnificent spectrum that lights the way to unity and development."

7. "In the garden of Bharat, respect will bloom in every corner—may the fruits of unity nurtured in diversity lead us to a thriving future."

8. "To achieve Viksit Bharat, we must see our diversity not as obstacles but as bridges, uniting us toward infinite possibilities."

1. "Incredible Bharat flourishes through the unity of dreams; each aspiration a brick, paving the path to Viksit Bharat."

2. "Vision is the blueprint; development is the architecture. Together, they construct the magnificent edifice of Incredible Bharat."

3. "As we cultivate innovation and nurture compassion, we plant the seeds of Viksit Bharat, blossoming into a garden of endless opportunities."

4. "In the tapestry of Incredible Bharat, every thread woven with purpose, resilience, and vision creates the beautiful narrative of development."

5. "The true essence of Viksit Bharat lies in the hearts of its people—a symphony of hope, ambition, and collective action."

6. "Let us rise as the architects of tomorrow, where Incredible Bharat transforms into a beacon of sustainable development for the world to behold."

7. "Incredible Bharat dreams beyond boundaries; with every step in innovation and equity, we awaken the potential of a Viksit future."

9 788199 862517

Printed at Repro India Ltd.